# PRACTICAL PISTOL

# PRACTICAL PISTOL

## Fundamental Techniques and Competition Skills

# BEN STOEGER

## Foreword by Ronnie Casper

Skyhorse Publishing

Skyhorse Publishing books may be purchased in bulk at special
discounts for sales promotion, corporate gifts, fund-raising, or
educational purposes. Special editions can also be created to
specifications. For details, contact the Special Sales Department,
Skyhorse Publishing, 307 West 36th Street, 11th Floor, New York,
NY 10018 or info@skyhorsepublishing.com.

Skyhorse® and Skyhorse Publishing® are registered trademarks of
Skyhorse Publishing, Inc.®, a Delaware corporation.

Visit our website at www.skyhorsepublishing.com.

Please follow our publisher Tony Lyons on Instagram
@tonylyonsisuncertain

10 9 8 7 6 5 4 3 2 1

Library of Congress Cataloging-in-Publication Data is available on file.

Print ISBN: 978-1-5107-7948-8
eBook ISBN: 978-1-5107-7949-5

Cover design by David Ter-Avanesyan
Cover photograph by Getty Images

Printed in China

# CONTENTS

# FOREWORD
## BY RONNIE CASPER

Assisting Ben with classes over the past few years, I usually start by telling students of my first experience with him.

I was filling in as Match Director at an IDPA Classifier match when this confident (some might say cocky) kid and his buddies arrived for our new shooter orientation class held prior to the match. Following a little instruction on range rules, the group all did well on their classifications. You can imagine my surprise (or shock) to be asked to sign Ben's classification card certifying him Master in two separate divisions. In what I'll describe as "typical Ben style," he did not seem all that impressed with his own performance and accepted his signed card with a yawn.

Ben became a regular fixture at our club and the other Wisconsin IDPA clubs. He and his buddies camped out in a small tent in the pouring rain just to shoot the state match, in which Ben ultimately won his division. In need of a new challenge, Ben turned to USPSA, since it had grown more widespread in our state, with us and others forming new clubs. This time I was not surprised in the least when he initially classified as Grand Master.

The following year we began shooting and practicing together, and Ben began attending larger matches. He did not always win these matches, but always placed well.

When he did win, he was not pleased with his performance and pointed out where he could have improved. This always drove him to practice harder, even the very next day after a large match. He once told me that he didn't win because of how well he performed, but because he didn't screw up as much as the next guy. He has always had an obsession with that unachievable perfect run.

Others began to take notice of Ben winning major matches and wanted to learn his secrets. Due to demand, he began teaching classes at our club. He was a little nervous at first (if you can believe), but eventually found his groove. Being self-taught with no formal training, Ben had a unique perspective on training and teaching. He studied every shooting-related book he could get his hands on and watched videos of "The Greats," such as Rob Leatham, shooting national competitions. He dry-fired in his basement for two hours every night and spent hours on shooting forums picking the brains of the best shooters, all while working and attending school. Ben had a unique analytical capability to take the best knowledge from every source and compile it, while disregarding what he considered to be useless information.

Ben's ability to "cut out the crap" rolled over into his teaching. He was brutally honest (to his own detriment at times) and did not hold back. When a student executed a drill incorrectly, Ben had the ability to see immediately what he felt they were doing wrong and pointed it out in a matter-of-fact way. Students came away from his classes knowing exactly what they were doing wrong and exactly how to fix it.

On the other hand, when a student was doing well in his class, it only provoked him to push them harder to find how fast they could go before "the wheels came off." Most people practice a technique until they are good at it, and then continue practicing to maintain what they have gained. Ben continues to raise the bar until the wheels come off. He continues raising the bar to the unattainable "perfect" run.

*Ronnie Casper*
*Wisconsin Section*
*Coordinator—USPSA*
*Grand Master*

I hope that through competing with him, taking a class, or even reading his books, you will find what you need to get to that next level.

# THE POINT

You didn't pick up this book by accident. You didn't confuse this book with a cookbook or a novel. You saw the sweet cover art (I hope it is sweet, I am writing this before anyone does the cover) and knew that this was a book about shooting. More specifically, this is the second edition of my book *Practical Pistol: Fundamental Techniques and Competition Skills*.

You are probably rightly wondering why I would rewrite the book. It has only been a few years since it came out, and it was pretty well received. Not to toot my own horn too much, but I received a lot of great feedback on the book. People liked how it was direct and easy to understand. I caught some flak for the "crappy" (my editor won't let me use words like s***, so I have to use PG substitutes) photos, but for the most part it went over well.

The book needs to be rewritten because I can make it better. I can make it a lot better. I have had a few more years of training, competition, and teaching experience. That experience is extremely valuable to a project like this. Not only do I know my own shooting better, but I have had thousands of people come through classes, each of them with a unique set of problems. I have also figured out better ways to communicate with those people. I have abandoned some of the ideas of *Practical Pistol* and replaced them with new ones. This new *Practical Pistol* will reflect that.

I have built this book as a "from the ground up" study of handgun shooting technique. The format isn't exactly new. This is how you hold the gun. This is how you press the trigger. This is how you do whatever. You can skip to the stuff you find interesting, or you can read it from start to finish. You will probably have a better understanding if you go from the beginning all the way to the end, but I would guess that the people who would benefit most from that recommendation skipped this section anyways. One thing writing a few books has taught me is that people often buy them, but rarely read them. Fine by me, I guess.

Obviously, this book is intended for the competitive shooter. If you are interested in tactical shooting, then this may not be the book for you. On the other hand, you may find some of the techniques in here invaluable. In any event, I personally have little interest in "tactical" shooting. The contents of the book will reflect that. Of course, many people are interested in both competition and tactical shooting, and there is obviously nothing wrong with that. They will take the stuff they like from this book and leave the rest.

If you are interested more in tactical training, concealed carry, or self-defense, then you might want to pick up *T.A.P.S. Tactical Application of Practical Shooting.* This is a book written by Pat McNamara on exactly the topic of using practical shooting concepts and applying those concepts to self-defense training.

**Inside this book, however, I will:**

**Explain the fundamentals:** I will explain the fundamentals of every technique. I like lists. I use a lot of them. The "fundamentals" are the things that must happen in order for you to accomplish an objective. For example, you need to aim the gun at a target, and then press the trigger without moving the gun in order to hit that target. In bullet point format, it would be this:

1.  Aim at target
2.  Press trigger without moving the gun

Pretty clear right? After I give you the bullet points, I will then explain the ins and outs of everything. I will answer the "why?" questions.

**Explain the "best" way to perform the technique:** I will explain the "best" techniques as I understand them. You may be wondering why best is in quotation marks. Am I implying that these techniques are not in fact the best? It is a tricky subject to address. There is so much disagreement about any topic you could care to mention in the shooting world and so many different understandings. Therefore, I hesitate to say that anything I am doing is definitively the "best" way to do it. Let's be honest, I am completely overhauling a book I wrote on the subject after only three years! Things change. Ideas change. Be ready to be a student for life if you want to be a great pistol shooter.

**Point out mistakes:** I will point out some of the most common mistakes that people make when it comes to a specific technical area. I have made every mistake in the book, (literally) except for shooting myself. I have not done that yet.

My point is, I am going to point out many common issues that shooters have. Throwing the gun up over the target when you draw (fishing) is a very common mistake. You have probably heard of it. There is a plethora of other mistakes that people make on a regular basis, but they are subtle and hard to detect unless you know what to look for. I will give you some hints about what to be looking for.

**Set the bar:** I will give you benchmarks for technique. What is a "good" grip or a "good" draw? What sort of times should I be able to achieve when reloading? I have answers to those questions.

**Give a method to improve:** Although this isn't a drill book, I want to offer a few tips and practice exercises so you know how to improve your shooting.

**Other issues:** There are some ideas, terminology, and techniques that aren't present in this book. I have a section explaining why many of those things aren't included and why you shouldn't miss most of them.

**Other opinions:** This book contains a few blurbs written by other practical shooting Grand Masters: Bob Vogel, Matthew Mink, Dave Sevigny, Keith Garcia, Blake Miguez, JJ Racaza, Mike Hughes, Brad Engmann,

Chris Bartolo, Taran Butler, Jay Hirshberg, and Matthew Hopkins. They have all been generous enough with their time to give some additional insights on different topics. I made a point of having them write what they think about something without me getting in the middle of it. Some of them don't agree with me on everything. That is totally fine. Again, take what you like and forget about the stuff you don't.

The techniques named and described in this book may not be named in ways you have previously heard. This is not done to confuse you (I promise). A big problem in the field of shooting technique is that all sorts of people talk about all sorts of different techniques using all sorts of different terminology. Different instructors may use the same term to mean different things. Some people say they use a certain technique (as it is commonly understood), but in fact, use a slightly different variation of that technique. At the end of the day, the terminology used doesn't really matter that much. I could call my draw technique "banana" and your draw technique "elephant" if I wanted to. That isn't the point. The idea here is to read past the name and understand the details.

The techniques in this book are organized in roughly the order I would teach and talk about them in a class, with a few exceptions. I also make mention of a few topics in one section that may seemingly fit better in another section, but due to the way different techniques intertwine, I made a decision to move these topics around for clarity. You should probably read the whole thing in order to get a good understanding of what I am talking about, but again, I am not your mom.

I will discuss speed and accuracy through the lens of USPSA shooting. USPSA has its own scoring system, and it is complex. Simply put, you want to score as many points as you can, as fast as you can. You are required to shoot a full power handgun in USPSA. There is no airsoft or .22 rimfire. The specifics aren't all that important when discussing fundamentals.

Some shooters or trainers may criticize certain techniques found in this book as being too difficult to learn. They may be difficult to learn, but shooters that practice a lot develop these techniques. A technique being difficult to learn or understand is not usually a consideration so long as it is otherwise the most effective. Competitive shooters are going to do thousands upon thousands of repetitions of any given technique during training anyway if they want to do well. If any given shooter needs to do 10,000 repetitions of a drill to get a tiny increase in their match score, it is worth it.

I have a few smaller sections at the back of the book that scratch the surface of different topics. IDPA shooting, Open guns, and equipment all are touched on. That information isn't comprehensive, but it is a good start down the road.

The most important caveat of this whole opening section is that this book is technique according to Ben (and a few others). I have opinions on technique that you may find unconventional or maybe even crazy. That is OK. This isn't gospel being handed down from the mountain; this is a pistol shooting book. Take it with a grain of salt.

With all that being said, let's get on with the show.

# USPSA CHALLENGES

As I laid out for you in "The Point" section, this book has a very specific aim. I am concerned with handgun techniques for the specific application of USPSA handgun competition. I want to produce the fastest times and best scores with the most consistency possible. Basically, I want to smash as much face as consistently as possible.

If you know little or nothing about USPSA and somehow stumbled onto this book, I should take a bit of time to explain to you what USPSA is and why it is awesome.

A USPSA match is kind of like a golf course. Every hole on the course is called a "stage" in the match. Most club level matches have four to six stages. If you go to a major match, they usually have more like fifteen stages. The interesting thing is that the stages contain a variety of different shooting challenges. The targets may be five feet away. They may be 50 yards away. It is different every time. Some stages require you to shoot prone; others require you to shoot one-handed. Some require lots of running around to be able to get to all the targets. Diversity is a big deal in USPSA shooting. (I mean diversity in a shooting sense; as far as actual diversity goes, USPSA is mostly middle-aged white dudes.)

The scoring system is another interesting feature of USPSA. It is a little bit complicated, some people would say insanely complicated, but it can be summed up simply. Your score is determined by dividing your points by the time it takes you to shoot the stage. So . . . the faster you go, the better. The more accurate you are, the better. The top guys are fast enough that they are going to be shooting so fast it is hard to believe they are actually aiming and accurate enough that they don't miss a whole lot. It is a competitive sport and very challenging to do well.

Therefore, if you are somehow reading this without having competed at a USPSA match, I want you to remember what this book is all about. That is, shooting fast and accurately at the same time.

# STUDENT OF THE SPORT

Before I get into the technique of shooting, I want to take some time to implore every reader to become a student of USPSA shooting. Obviously, it takes time, ammunition, and training to become the best you can be in USPSA. Just as important as those things is using your brain.

So many shooters just go through the motions. "Doing your dry-fire" for thirty minutes a day is a good thing. Of course it is. However, if you don't engage your brain, then you are going to very quickly get to a point where you aren't getting better. Don't be lazy. Figure out why.

This book or any other resource that you use shouldn't be something that you read once, and then discard. This is something you should study. As you improve and grow as a shooter, your understanding will change, and you will be able to glean new and different things from rereading the same text.

As you learn how to transition faster between targets, you may have questions about sight alignment. As you work on grip strength, you may have issues with trigger control. Every time you move forward with your shooting, then more questions will come up. Don't stop finding the answers.

This is a self-help book. Help yourself to get better. Engage your brain. Become a student.

## From Nick Yanutola (USPSA Grand Master, "Top 16" finisher at Production Nationals)

### Mental Approach

*When Ben asked me for a brief contribution to the second edition of* Practical Pistol, *I thought for a time about what I could possibly add in terms of shooting knowledge base that was not already excellently covered in other parts of the book. Eventually, I decided to go a different route, and add some comments about the mindset it takes to really improve—from the perspective of someone who once had to make serious changes in that area, in order to*

*progress. In an amateur sport such as USPSA, because there are so few true professionals, all but a tiny handful of people in the entire world can see major gains if they are able to* change their mindset for the better. We often hear that "the game is 90 percent mental." I believe that to be true. So how can we improve? I will outline what I feel are two key aspects of the mental approach to the game: accountability and priority.

What does being accountable mean? It means that everything matters, all the time. There are no mulligans. You are the sum of everything you do that is related to this sport. You own what you do in practice. You own what you do in club matches. You own what you do in major matches—at every match, on every stage, every time. If you can't own your mistakes, you can't really hope to correct them.

How do you apply this concept in practice? Mistakes, especially in practice, are, of course, inevitable. When you are pushing skills to new levels, there are going to be many instances when you screw up. This is good, since it means you are finding your limits in practice, and then working to push them further. You have to have a goal, and you can't be "OK" with the delta between your current performance, and where you want to be. Your accountability here is to be motivated and organized above all else. That delta has to gnaw at the pit of your stomach and be your motivation to continue on.

At club matches, we've all seen (and have likely been at one time) the guy that trashes a stage, walks off, and says "Well, I was rusty because I haven't been getting my practice in lately. That isn't me. That doesn't really count. I'll get 'em next time. I'll be ready by the time the state championship rolls around." That is not being accountable. I have bad news: in that moment, that is you. You just *did that. We all make mistakes, but the best shooters do a better job of acknowledging a mistake, owning it, and committing to do whatever it takes to correct it regardless of where, when, or how it occurred. It matters not whether it occurred on the first stage of the day, at the first club match of the year, or at the national championship. You are accountable for how you prepare and perform, always.*

*The second aspect of the mental approach I mentioned above is "priority." I believe there is an axiom that is very useful when describing how priority is important to you in your development as a shooter. It comes from the world of financial investing: If you want to build wealth reliably, the number one rule is to always, without fail, "pay yourself first." What does that mean in real world application? It means that your nest egg is your highest financial priority. When you receive income, you put a pre-determined percentage into savings immediately, and then you spend or live on what is left. Doing the opposite (spending first, and saving what is left) is a great way to hardly ever save a dime.*

*The same concept applies to improving as a shooter. Virtually all of us have jobs or family obligations that dominate our time, and that is fine, and virtually unavoidable. But, you will never maximize your potential as a shooter until you can maximize the time priority that you put toward improving. Once you've set shooting goals, you also need to allocate time to practice, be it dry-fire or live-fire. Then, when you make free time in your life, you must "pay yourself first" by investing that time in improvement. When you get home from work, getting your dry-fire reps in is your top priority, not something that you might get to after TV is watched or the grass* is cut. When the weekend rolls around, live-fire is getting done, period. If it overlaps with the game or whatever else, you can catch the highlights later. You must consistently "pay yourself first" with regard to time commitments and regular practice when pressing toward aggressive shooting goals, or you will simply never get there. Using "leftover time" is not an option for someone who wishes to attain GM level in this sport. As with anything else worth doing, you can't expect to get more out of the sport than you are willing to put in.

So remember to suck it up, buttercup . . . and I will see you on the range!

*About Nick:*

Nick has been dedicated to competing as hard as possible in pistol sports for the last several years. He has a total of eleven years' experience in IDPA and four years' experience in USPSA. Nick is a Production Grand Master and completed the 2014 and 2015 seasons as a "Top 16" finisher at USPSA Production National Championships.

**From Gaston Quindi Vallerga (Argentine National Champion and has won the Florida Open and Pan American titles)**

Some guys are touched with the wonder stick, the rest of us just have to train as hard as hell to get there, because God

*only gave us the will. If you are one of the rest of us mortals, then you will need tons of information and training. Some may say I was a naturally accurate guy, but that's not true. I trained hundreds of thousands of rounds to master my accuracy, so I did spend time and money training . . . a lot. . . . I am a very egocentric guy and I always refused to seek aid from other top shooters or study any bibliographic material; I figured out nobody would share real valuable information, though I always did share it with my students. So, I´m not embarrassed to say, I almost built up all my actual technique out of nothing. In fact, the first guy that gave me very valuable information regarding accuracy was Frank Garcia, in my own club. I managed to become a top gamer in Latin America, thanks to his info, but it still was not enough to convince me to reach for help. My speed was not OK, and I really didn't trust top gamers would ever teach me that which I lacked to beat them. So, I started studying top gamer's movements with a professional sports analyzer, and we both agreed JJ Racazza and Eric Grauffel were the perfect guys to study. We developed together a refined movements method that especially suited me, but I was still always a nick away from glory. Though I ruled Latin America, had some great matches in Europe, won some major USPSA matches in the US, became Top 10 at USPSA NATIONALS 2014 and become a Distinguished Master in IDPA, I still felt something was missing. Then,*

*Ben entered in my life. I like straightforward guys, so we became close friends really quick, and I was specially surprised about his humbleness. He knows and respects his own limitations, that's why he is constantly evolving. We shot several matches together, always discussing technique issues. At the last US IPSC NATIONALS he told me "Gaston, I want to visit Buenos Aires and I want you to help me train." And he did. I will never forget when I was telling him about human reaction response, and analyzing some of my own shooting theories, developed thanks to my knowledge about human reaction that I learned while doing my Forensic Scientist Degree, when he suddenly interrupts me and tells me my own theory in his own words and I said . . . "Wow . . . you already knew this???? I thought you were just a natural shooter . . ." So Ben gives me his watch, like saying you idiot . . . and so he tells me "Gaston . . . I'm an expert in my field. Didn't you read any of the books I sent you?" And it was there, every single thing I knew and figured out by myself, was in his book . . . At that moment, I realized that I had wasted years of study, when information was at hands reach. Somebody did really put ALL THAT IS NEEDED TO KNOW to became a top shooter, in a bunch of books. Ben is not only an expert at teaching because he knows how to shoot, he is an expert in his field because he saves nothing for himself, not even from a guy like me, that is not far away from beating him. So . . . it doesn't matter how much you suck, if there's a will, there's a book and a man that can help you. Ben Stoeger.*

# MARKSMANSHIP FUNDAMENTALS

I am beginning the discussion of technique with the most important thing. "Marksmanship Fundamentals" is simply a fancy way of saying "hitting a target in the center."

**Fundamentals**

1. Align the muzzle of the gun with the target.
2. Hold that alignment until you discharge the firearm.

That's it. So simple right?

I am going to do what I promised now. You have your main points, and I am going to explain each point to the last detail. I have to warn you; this section is going to get complicated. I am going to explain, in detail, how most matches are going to be decided based on marksmanship fundamentals. It is just going to take a bit of work to get a thorough explanation in place.

For now, let's say that the fundamentals of marksmanship are to aim at the target, then to pull the trigger without disturbing that aim. Notice this is really close to what I listed in the bullet points above, but it isn't quite the same. I will come back around to that later because the difference is subtle, but ultimately quite important.

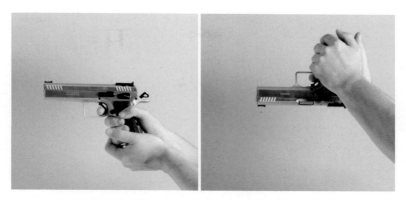

*Marksmanship fundamentals can be executed no matter how you hold the gun.*

In shooting, as in life, context is pretty much everything. I want to put my discussion of marksmanship fundamentals in context, so you understand the key points I am going to be making about it. I am going to discuss context in terms of three things. I want to talk about shooting slowly without measuring the time. I am also going to talk about shooting a single target at regular USPSA match speed. Finally, I want to talk about shooting multiple targets under actual match pressure at a real match. Every situation is a bit different.

## Slow Fire Shooting

First, I want to talk about marksmanship in the context of no time limit shooting. This is probably what you are envisioning when I start talking about marksmanship. Let me give you a goal for this type of shooting. Hitting the "A" zone every single shot at 25 yards with no time limit is a fair goal. Your gun ought to be able to do that. YOU ought to be able to do that.

Hitting the "A" zone at 25 yards is straightforward. You aim the gun at the target ("Marksmanship Fundamentals" Number 1), then press the trigger without moving anything ("Marksmanship Fundamentals" Number 2). In my experience, people screw up "Number 2" about 10 times more often than they screw up "Number 1."

There are many reasons for this. A gun going off in front of your face is disconcerting if you aren't used to it. People have a strong inclination to blink, flinch, jerk the trigger, or all sorts of other things that disturb the aim of the gun. The trick is to pull the trigger straight back without doing anything else. The blast and recoil make it hard to tell if you moved the gun slightly off target at the time the shot went off. This is not dissimilar to trying to have a conversation in a loud bar. The music and noise can drown out a conversation.

There are many factors (such as grip, stance, and breathing) that can have some play in marksmanship, but they are insignificant compared to the ability to fire the gun without moving it. You may be worried about whether to focus on the front sight or the target. You may be wondering how to hold the gun. The truth is, it isn't going to matter all that much when you are shooting without a time limit. Have you ever seen a picture of a bullseye match? Old men, shooting one-handed, while wearing blinders are able to hit targets 50 yards away. The key is that they don't need to go fast.

If you have an issue pressing the trigger straight, there are a couple things you can try:

The most common method of correcting the blink/flinch/jerk problem is something usually referred to as the "surprise trigger break." The idea behind this is that the shooter trains to pull the trigger slowly in such a way that the gun "surprises" the shooter when it goes off. If the shooter is surprised, they can't possibly jerk the trigger in anticipation of the blast or recoil, because they didn't know that the recoil was going to happen right at that moment.

The "surprise trigger break" is trained in a few ways. The primary method is something that is usually referred to as the "ball and dummy" drill. What the shooter does is load their magazines in such a way that they mix in a bunch of inert (dummy) ammunition with the live ammunition. If they have a friend load their magazines for them, they won't know where the dummy rounds are situated in the magazine. I also enjoy playing the ball and dummy game without telling my friend we are going to play. What happens as someone shoots with dummy rounds in the magazine is that eventually they get a dummy round in the chamber, pull the trigger, and see the gun move without a round being fired. This is a good way to illustrate someone's flinch to them. Once someone can feel their flinch, they tend to be able to correct it quickly.

This sort of training is fine, but it limits you to slow fire shooting. Remember that I said in shooting, context is pretty much everything. When you move on to shooting quickly, you aren't going to have time to press the trigger slowly and let the gun surprise you when it goes off. Not to mention, when you shoot your gun enough, you are going to learn the trigger to the point that it is going to be very difficult to surprise yourself when the gun goes off.

I have found the most logical goal is to be able to shoot the gun you have, as well as that gun will mechanically shoot.

What that means for most Production-type guns is something less than a four-inch group at 25 yards. There are many variables with different types of guns and different types of ammunition, but a four-inch group should be attainable from most combinations. Some guns will do a lot better. A bit of research on the particulars of your gun will give you a good benchmark for what you should be striving for.

There is one more point I simply must make. For the entirety of my USPSA career, I have been striving to shoot more accurately. I have become a lot better at simply hitting the target in that time. However, no matter how much I train, I never feel accurate enough.

### The Phantom Flinch

*One interesting phenomenon that occurs occasionally is that a very well-trained and skilled shooter will be firing a high-speed string of shots, and then for some reason (malfunction, out of ammunition, etc.), pull the trigger expecting a shot to be fired, but no shot will happen. When the shooter pulls the trigger expecting a shot, they will push down on the gun and this will appear to be a severe flinch. If this truly is a well-trained shooter, it won't be a flinch at all. The shooter will push down on the gun to control the recoil, but they will push at the moment just after the trigger is pulled. This is a key distinction. Pushing the gun down after the shot breaks is recoil control (sometimes called "timing" or "driving the gun"); pushing it down just before the shot breaks is a flinch.*

## Shooting Fast

When we discuss "marksmanship fundamentals" in the context of shooting fast, then things change. No longer do you have time to slowly press the trigger to the rear and carefully watch the gun go off. You need to go! You need to lay shots non-stop on the target.

Other parts of your technique will start to matter. How you stand matters. How you grip the gun matters. Those topics will be covered in detail in the relevant sections of the book. For now, just recognize that when you start shooting fast, you need to do some work to get the gun back on target, ready to go for the next shot. All that work you are doing translates into a bunch of tension in your hands. That makes it infinitely harder to press the trigger straight back. The muscles in your trigger finger are difficult to isolate from the rest of your hand. It is hard to feel exactly what is happening because of all the recoil in addition to the pressure you are feeling to go fast.

Of course, people also have problems with aiming when they are shooting fast. Generally speaking, they either don't wait to get a sight picture on a target before they start shooting or they don't wait for the sight picture to return before firing the next shot at that target.

It boils down to a high-speed coordination of your eyes, hands, and trigger finger. You put the sights between your eye and the target, and press the trigger straight back while not letting all the tension in your body disturb the process.

If you want to demonstrate this to yourself, take your unloaded gun and point it at a target. If you take your time and press the trigger straight, you should be able to drop the hammer or striker without having the sights move. If you see the front sight wiggle at all, then you made a mistake. Most people can press the trigger without anything moving in an unloaded gun in the space of 10 or 20 practice repetitions. Simply put, this isn't hard to do.

However, if you point the same unloaded gun at the same target, then press the trigger as fast as you possibly can, you are going to have a much harder time keeping everything still. This essentially is the crux of the problem. When you are going fast, gripping the gun hard, fighting recoil, and under match pressure, it is tough to press the trigger straight.

Dry-firing will give you the "feeling" of pulling the trigger straight back. It is essential to know how it feels, and a great way to learn that feeling is to skip using ammunition for a while, so you can figure it out. It is easier for many people to think of pulling the trigger as "pressing" the trigger. If you are having a problem moving the trigger straight back, then try changing how you conceptualize it.

Every shooter needs to learn this skill. People may differ on the specific technique for how to manipulate the trigger straight to the rear (more on that in the "Trigger Control" section). Make no mistake; the best shooters in the game have mastered the fundamentals.

### White Wall Drill
*The idea is that you dry-fire (with an unloaded firearm, of course) at a white wall. You don't want a specific target on the wall. You don't want to aim at a bump or a spot on*

*the wall. You simply work with your sights against a plain white canvas. You practice manipulating the trigger so the sights simply do not move. Essentially, you are learning the "feel" of pulling the trigger straight back and getting visual feedback from your sights at the same time. You can train pressing the trigger faster and faster while still pressing it straight back. When you go out to the range to shoot live rounds, you can occasionally unload your gun and dry-fire some more (this time using the target) to remember the "feel" of firing a shot without disturbing the sights. I have observed shooters make dramatic improvement in a single range session when using this method with none of the drawbacks associated with the "surprise break" technique.*

## Shooting a Real Match

When shooting multiple targets at a real match, things get even tougher. No longer do you only need to focus on trigger control to hit things, but the element of multiple targets along with the speed makes things even tougher.

For example, it is common to pull the gun off target while in a hurry to get to the next target. I suppose this error would fall under the second fundamental, but it is a different thing than flinching or jerking the trigger.

Other times, people will throw the gun toward a target in an effort to hit it quickly, but they will never really aim the gun at the target. They just pointed at it and didn't get things lined up properly. Again, this mistake would fall under the first fundamental, but it isn't exactly the same thing as having the sights a bit misaligned.

My point is this:

At the core, USPSA competition is about high-speed coordination. You find the target, aim at the target, shoot, recover your sight picture, shoot again, and then acquire the next target. Usually, you are going to be doing several of these steps each second. This all needs to be coordinated on a subconscious level. The speed of it is going to make executing the fundamentals difficult, but at the core there is nothing complicated happening.

As you read the rest of this book, keep these fundamentals in mind. Everything you are going to do will relate to these fundamentals in some important way. Gripping the gun better helps the gun recover faster. Transitioning the gun precisely to the next target will make it easier to be accurate. Working on your trigger control will keep the gun stable as you shoot. The more elements you add in to your shooting, and the faster you go, the greater the possibility for mistakes enters into the equation. Layering one technique on top of another, multiplied by speed, is a recipe for confusion. You must never forget that when you get confused about some error you are making, you need to figure out what the fundamental problem is and sort it out.

# GRIP

I think if I had to pick one thing that I most often correct people on in a class; it would be gripping their pistol. Before I get too far down the road of discussing the ins and outs of how to grip the gun and the different schools of thought on it, I would like to get the benefits of a good grip out of the way.

Gripping your gun very firmly is going to offer you quite a bit of recoil control. The gun is going to behave very nicely for you in recoil. The sights lift and return to the same spot. You are able to shoot at a close-range five-yard target as fast as you can pull the trigger and make a group about the size of a softball. Just to be clear about this, the way you control the recoil of your gun is with your hands, not with anything else. Leaning into the gun more isn't going to help a whole lot. Hyperextending your elbows won't really matter, and tensing up your shoulder muscles won't help. You control the recoil of the gun primarily with your hands and that's it.

Aside from recoil control, a firm grip also helps as a crutch against poor trigger control. If you put pressure into the trigger a little bit sideways, or not quite straight back in to the frame, then normally the shot will move slightly off target. However, if you are holding the gun like a vise, then a little bit of sideways pressure will not be a huge deal to you.

With the benefits of a great grip apparent, let's talk about the elements that most credible shooters/instructors agree on:

1.  Grip the gun as high up as possible
2.  Utilize as much gripping surface as you can
3.  Grip the gun hard (really hard)
4.  Grip the gun in such a way that you minimize interference with the controls of the firearm
5.  Grip the gun the same way every time

At this point, I am going to go through each one of these fundamentals and talk about them individually and how they interact with each other. Just to warn you, this can get complicated and pedantic, but I feel it is important to offer answers to major questions that people have.

The first fundamental is to grip the gun as high up as possible. The reason for this is that the higher up you hold the gun, the more control you have over the gun when it is in recoil. This is easily demonstrated if you go to a shooting range and hold the gun extremely low. If you leave an inch or so between your dominant hand and the beavertail of the gun, you will see a dramatic amount of "muzzle flip" when you actually fire the gun. (Try not to hurt yourself if you conduct this little test.)

*Grip the gun as high up as possible (side view).*

This should go without saying, but I am sure my lawyer will make me say it anyway. Don't grip the gun so high that you end up hurting yourself. Stay well clear of the slide. Stay clear of the controls of the gun. You want to be far enough away from all the moving parts of the gun that you aren't going to get bitten by the slide or any other part.

This brings us to the second grip fundamental. It is important to use as much gripping surface as you possibly can. The reasoning behind this is simple: the more of the gun you make contact with, the more control you are going to have over it. This is the same reason that fast cars have wider tires. More contact with the road means more control.

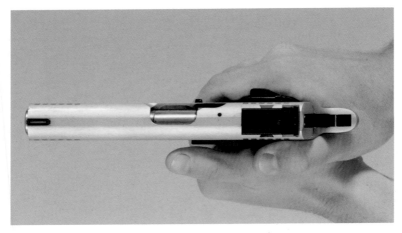

*Grip the gun as high up as possible (top view).*

The scenario in which I see people most commonly have an issue with not making contact with the gun all the way around the gripping surface is when they are using a gun that doesn't fit them. Not to pick on anyone, but I commonly see this when there is a dude with big hands using a CZ-75 (or one of the variants) with aftermarket thin grips. This means that the dude's strong hand will wrap around most of the gun, but there isn't enough space for him to get his non-dominant hand into the gripping surface part of the gun . . . at least not without quite a bit of effort. You simply can't grip the gun as effectively if you are leaving a big chunk of the gun un-gripped.

All of this ends up being a bit of a balancing act. Taking up a lot of grip surface is important, but so is being up high. You may be able to work your weak hand up the gun a bit higher, but not have quite the same amount of contact surface. Everyone's situation is a little bit different, but usually it is best to go with what is comfortable and consistent for you over what you think may be better in theory. For example, if you are shooting a Glock with an extended magazine release, you may find that when you get up on the gun as high as you possibly can, you are in contact with the magazine release a little bit. It digs into your hand, and you are concerned you may inadvertently drop magazines. Well, there is no harm in sidestepping the issue by dropping your non-dominant hand down a bit.

Another logical question at this point would be "how do I situate my non-dominant hand on the frame?"

I think the best way to conceptualize this is to push the "meat" of your non-dominant hand into the grip panel. Your dominant hand's thumb needs to be out of the way, (probably up off the gun, about even with the slide). That way your non-dominant hand is able to utilize the entire gripping surface available to you on that side of the gun.

For simplicity's sake, I personally prefer to put my non-dominant pointer finger against the bottom of the trigger guard. I teach gripping this way in classes because it integrates easily with drawing and reloading techniques. Draw the gun, run the side of the pointer finger on your non-dominant hand in to the bottom of the trigger guard, and use that as a reference point to line your hand up on the frame. The same works when you reload. After seating the magazine, then run the side of your pointer finger into the bottom of the frame, and use that as a reference point for when you re-grip the pistol (I will discuss reloads in depth later). I think this is the easiest system to learn and to use, so if you don't have a system for gripping the pistol consistently, then I recommend that you try this one. If you prefer to roll your hands further up the trigger guard, then that of course is totally fine by me, I just like to have a system to offer to people that aren't really sure yet.

### Finger on the Trigger Guard

*Some more astute readers might point out that it is possible to get the non-dominant hand up even higher on the gun by hooking the pointer finger of that hand around the trigger guard. This is not a popular technique in USPSA circles, but some extremely well trained shooters do utilize the technique. A couple of shooters that I know use this technique, but strongly advise their students NOT to use it. The reason for this disconnect is that it is the general opinion of many shooters that hooking the non-dominant pointer finger on the front of the trigger guard can cause an issue called "steering." Pressure applied by that finger in any direction other than straight back toward the trigger can influence the muzzle of the gun off target. The potential upside is (just as I pointed out) you are situated a bit higher on the gun for recoil control purposes. Depending on the particulars of your gun, you may have to grip the gun slightly different with your non-dominant hand's palm, and this may reduce overall grip effectiveness. Overall, hooking the non-dominant hand's pointer finger on the trigger guard doesn't offer any serious advantage over the more popular and conventional technique, but with training can be effective.*

Let's talk about the third grip fundamental, "Grip the gun hard." It is intuitively figured out by even the novice shooter that the harder they grip the gun, the less it moves.

If you aren't sure whether you are gripping the gun as hard as you should be, I offer you this simple test:

Are you gripping the gun as hard as you possibly can?
Circle one: Yes / No
If you circled "No," then grip the gun harder.
Simple right?

As a joke, it works pretty well, but the reality is a little bit more complicated.

For grip pressure, obviously more is better. It is going to help us control the gun. However, there is such a thing as too much grip pressure. Some people start shaking and holding the gun unsteadily if they grip absolutely as hard as they can. Sometimes gripping as hard as possible with your dominant hand will contribute to trigger control problems.

As tempting as it is for me to say, "Grip the gun hard as F***," then move on to the next topic; there are some complicated issues that we need to talk about here.

First, I think it is easier to separate your hands. Your dominant hand and your non-dominant hand each have different jobs to do. Obviously, one of them is pulling the trigger and the other one isn't. For this reason, I think you can treat them a little bit differently.

For your non-dominant hand, I think gripping the gun absolutely as hard as you can is a bit more realistic. When you grip as hard as you can, you tend to lose a bit of dexterity in your hand. That won't matter because you aren't pulling the trigger with that hand.

With your dominant hand, that loss of dexterity could be a problem. When you press the trigger, you want the trigger to move and nothing else. That can be a tough proposition when you are gripping the gun 100 percent as hard as you can with your dominant hand. For that reason, I find it easiest for most people to back off a little bit and just hold on to the gun with that hand.

I think this sort of thing is the reason that I have heard about the 60/40 IPSC grip or maybe the 70/30 grip. Having the hands grip the gun with different amounts of force seems like it makes sense from a dexterity standpoint, so that is the reason that you have probably heard these different grip percentages thrown around.

I think the easiest way to do it is to grip the gun with your dominant hand . . . grip it firmly. The old advice of holding it like you would hold a hammer to pound in a nail makes sense. With your non-dominant hand, crush the gun. Pretend the gun is someone you don't like if that helps you, whatever. Just crush the snot out of the gun with your non-dominant hand, because that is where you are going to get most of the control over the gun.

I should point out that if you are able to grip the gun harder with your strong hand and not have it cause problems for you, then by all means do it. Most students I get in a class that are having problems with grip, tend to start "over gripping" with their strong hand, when they are put under time pressure during high-speed close range shooting. This usually results in "trigger freeze" as they lose the dexterity in their dominant hand trigger finger and are unable to reset the trigger.

So, just to quickly recap this. Grip the gun as hard as you can without causing problems. If your dominant hand is so tense that you can't work the trigger fast and straight, then back off a bit. If your non-dominant hand starts shaking, then back off a bit. Otherwise, grip away. Just to give you an idea of how hard I personally grip: I regularly remove skin from the back of my dominant hand with my non-dominant hand because of the force I am gripping with.

The fourth grip fundamental is to not interfere with the controls of your firearm. This may seem silly, but it is a big problem for certain people and certain guns. For example, Sig 226's are widely regarded as having a slide stop that is very easy to inadvertently push down on while firing, which prevents the slide from locking back. Issues like that can't always be avoided depending on the person's physical anatomy and the way their specific gun is laid out. Sometimes considerations need to be made so that you aren't accidentally hitting buttons you don't want to hit or if you're interfering with the movement of the slide. It is a normal thing to need to make certain concessions with grip technique because of equipment. These issues aren't exactly uncommon, and I need to leave them to you to solve on your own.

The fifth and final grip fundamental I proposed was that you must grip the gun the same way every single time. In the "Index" section you will learn about one of the benefits of having a consistent grip, but I think in the "Grip" section it definitely bears mentioning that you should pick a gripping technique or a piece of equipment that makes it easier to be consistent. Certain magwells may give you a good index point on the gun. A thumb rest will give you a consistent place to put your thumb, etc.

I think the key point I want to make about consistency, is that consistency is maybe even more important than grip strength. You absolutely must grip the gun the same way every single time.

With the theory side of things out of the way, let's move on to some common mistakes that people make.

The most common issue I see regarding grip is that shooters don't grip hard enough with their non-dominant hand. When someone has a proper grip and good control of their gun, the gun doesn't move around a whole lot when they shoot. If you watch closely, you will see that although the gun doesn't move much, it is locked into both of the shooters hands. The amazing thing about this to me is that some people will get pretty good at shooting USPSA, and get used to having really poor control of their gun. I can't even count how many B class guys I have met that don't control their gun that well, but they are so used to it that it doesn't bother them. It is like having a really overbearing girlfriend and you don't realize what a total nightmare she was until she is out of your life. You may be gripping the gun terribly and not even know it! Do yourself a favor. Go to the range, and try gripping as hard as you possibly can while just firing rounds into the berm. If you see the sights behave dramatically better for you, then you have some work to do on your grip.

Another really common error that I see people make when it comes to gripping the gun, is to grip the gun much more loosely when they are shooting at long distance targets or when they are shooting from an awkward position. I am not sure why, but it seems to be a natural tendency for people when they start shooting from a crouch or a lean to end up loosening up on the grip. Make certain you don't do that.

Finally, another common gripping mistake I see is that people end up getting "trigger freeze" during their close range/ high-speed shooting. I did briefly mention this earlier, but I think it bears some more explanation. I think what is happening here is that when people start rushing and wanting to "go fast," they start tensing up their bodies in an effort to make that speed happen. Often, this results in an overly tense dominant hand and some trigger freeze. I think the best prescription for this sort of problem is to do lots of close-range shooting during your training, with an emphasis on keeping yourself relaxed as much as you can. If your body tenses up too much, you will make mistakes.

If you recall, I mentioned earlier that a side benefit of a really good grip is that it is sort of a crutch against poor trigger control. That may seem like an obtuse proposition so I want to take a bit of time to explain what I mean.

A typical pistol that people use might weigh a couple of pounds. Sometimes it weighs a bit more and sometimes a bit less. This may sound like quite a bit of weight, but compared with the amount of force required to discharge the gun, it really isn't a lot. A trigger straight from the factory on a Glock, or something similar, is usually going to require more than five pounds of force to discharge. Even if you do a fairly typical "trigger job" modification to the gun and drop that weight down to three pounds, you will still need to apply more force to the trigger than the gun actually weighs in order to get the gun to go off. As you probably realized during the discussion of marksmanship fundamentals, the slightest movement of the gun when the shot is being fired can cause serious problems downrange. It is very easy to apply force to the trigger in a way that moves the muzzle, especially when you start shooting quickly.

One way to mitigate the effects of applying pressure to the trigger, such that it moves the muzzle (even slightly) and misaligns the gun as I described, is to have that hard grip that I talked about. This hard grip will not make a shooter impervious to poor trigger control, it will just make the "bad" trigger presses not quite as bad. Just to be clear, this doesn't mean that having a good grip is a requirement for accurate shooting when proper trigger control is utilized. This only means that a proper grip will aid in the trigger control department.

Finally, I think many experienced shooters are probably wondering where the discussion of the "straight thumbs" hold is. It is popular in USPSA circles to talk about pointing the thumbs straight at the target. I have experimented with this on many occasions and have never been able to produce any sort of effect by doing this. I have come to believe that the "straight thumbs" hold is popular because it naturally occurs with many shooters that use 1911s and 1911-style firearms. This "straight thumbs" thing isn't a grip fundamental and doesn't seem to have any effect on the grip itself.

Right along with the "straight thumbs" hold, I suspect a few people are wondering where the "locking your wrists" part comes in. I don't really know quite what people mean when they say "lock your wrists." I don't know that your wrists have a biological locking mechanism. When you grip hard, you are still able to move your wrists, so I suppose I don't really understand the advice.

Another issue I sometimes get questions about is what to do with your thumbs. It is common for shooters to want to use their thumbs to hold the gun. That is fine for the dominant hand. The thumb on that hand generally isn't in a position to cause any problems if that pressure goes straight into the frame. Many guns have a safety that a shooter can have their dominant hand "ride" to ensure it is disengaged and give them a consistent spot to place their hand when they grip the gun. However, the non-dominant thumb tends to be in a position that if you apply pressure straight into the gun, the thumb can interfere with the operation of the slide. Some shooters also "steer" the muzzle of the gun with the non-dominant thumb (similar to what can happen by putting your finger on the trigger guard). I think the best advice I can give is that if you aren't sure what to do with your non-dominant thumb, just keep it off the gun. You can of course learn to have it in contact with the gun if you want, but there isn't going to be much benefit to it. If you are concerned about it causing problems, you might as well just take it out of the equation.

Now that I have established, essentially, what a proper grip should look like, I can turn my attention to improving your grip.

As I pointed out in the fifth grip fundamental, it is absolutely critical that you grip your gun the same way every single time. You need to do this at speed, under pressure, with your friends watching. That isn't always an easy thing to pull off. The best recommendation that I have to assist in learning your grip is to use a sharpie to make marks on your hands. Actually, you will need someone else to mark up your hands for you, because you will be holding the gun. In any event, grip the gun properly (make sure it is perfect) and then draw lines across your hands. Two lines are plenty. Just draw a line from one-hand to the other. When you get your grip again, you can carefully check to make sure the lines "line up" with each other. This is a good way to develop a consistent grip.

*You can put lines on your hands to help learn the grip.*

Another thing that bears discussion when we are talking about improving our grip is the use of grip strength trainers. "Captains of Crush®" or similar grip trainers are a popular solution to the gripping harder issue. In my opinion, training yourself to have stronger hands sidesteps the issue of developing a proper grip. They aren't the same thing. I have seen plenty of strong, burly men that have incredibly strong hands have a really bad grip on the pistol. That is because they aren't actually using the strength they have to grip the pistol properly. On the other hand,

I have had a few really petite women in class actually grip the gun as hard as they can and immediately see improvement in their shooting. I am not exactly recommending against developing strong hands here. I just want to point out that based on my observations; the problem usually isn't that someone doesn't have strong hands. The problem is that they aren't using the strength that they currently have to the best possible effect. Use grip trainers if you want to, just make sure you actually deploy your hand strength properly.

Finally, one question always seems to crop up when discussing grip and that is tracking the sights. Many people correctly recognize that how they grip the gun affects the way the sights move in recoil. The problem with this is that they want the sights to move in some specific way when the gun is in recoil (usually straight up and down). The fact is, it doesn't really matter. The point of a good grip is to be able to shoot as quickly as possible, and for that to happen the sights need to return quickly. How the sights move isn't really important. Most people with a good strong grip get the sights to move basically up and down, but that isn't a requirement for good shooting. The important thing is fast and consistent sight return.

# TRIGGER CONTROL

Pressing the trigger quickly without messing up the sight picture is the name of the game with trigger control. There are a few different schools of thought on how to best accomplish this. I plan to discuss the major ones.

Before I get into talking about "pin and reset" trigger control or "prepping" the trigger, I think I should point out that many of these techniques are just ways to conceptualize pressing the trigger straight on back. The reason that all of these different concepts are discussed is because some people find each one of them useful in some way. The most important thing to remember is that if there is some way of thinking or some mental strategy that helps you press the trigger straight, then by all means do that thing.

The technique that I think is most prevalent in USPSA is variously known as "pin and reset" or "reset riding." This technique is considered by many to be the fastest and/or the most accurate technique available.

Pin and reset is all about keeping the trigger finger in contact with the trigger at all times and minimizing the motion of the trigger finger. After a shot is fired, the shooter maintains contact with the trigger and then carefully lets the trigger out only as far as it is necessary to "reset" the trigger mechanism. The shooter then preps the trigger by pulling it back to the point just before the trigger is ready to discharge the gun.

Pin and reset trigger control is thought by many to allow for the fastest possible firing of shots, because the trigger finger is moving the absolute minimum possible distance. I suppose this seems pretty logical to just about everyone.

The other major, but substantially less popular technique for trigger control is called "trigger slapping," or sometimes, "trigger sweeping." I should point out up front that "trigger slapping" in terms of a trigger control technique is not the same thing as "slapping the trigger." It is common in terms of marksmanship fundamentals for shooters to refer to a bad shot as "slapping" the trigger. When the term slapping is used in that context, it means carelessly pulling the trigger back in such a fashion that it caused a bad shot to be fired. That is not what we are talking about here.

What "trigger slapping" does refer to in this context is letting your finger come off the trigger between shots. To fire the next shot, the shooter then re-applies pressure to the trigger to discharge the gun again.

Trigger slapping (the technique) draws a lot of criticism. Many shooters feel that trigger slapping is only effective on "gamer guns" (1911/2011s with sub two-pound triggers). This is false, as I will discuss in just a moment.

### "Flip and Press" Trigger Control

*There is another somewhat obscure trigger control technique that is actually more properly described as a variation of trigger slapping. It is called "flip and press."*

*This technique is taught primarily at the Rogers Shooting School. With this technique, the trigger is held to the rear after a shot is fired. When the shooter decides to fire another shot, they release the trigger forward (or "flip" it if you prefer) and then press it back. The finger coming off the trigger during the flip is not considered a problem. Of course, to learn the details of this technique you should attend a Rogers' class.*

Now that all the techniques are described, we can delve into the ongoing arguments about them. As I said before, the weight of opinion seems to be in favor of "pin and reset." Moving the trigger the minimum amount possible strikes most people as logical and efficient. It is said that people can shoot the best on target split times using this technique. It is not uncommon to hear of a shooter firing two shots on a close-range target with the time between shots being only .12 seconds. Many shooters credit this speed to the pin and reset method (although I think shooters using other methods can be just as fast).

### Prove It to Yourself
*If you want to do a little experiment at home that might shed some light on the idea of trigger speed versus finger movement, try the following: Make a fist and lay it on a table. Using your pointer finger of that hand, tap the table hard. Try to apply a few pounds of force to the table with every tap. While you are doing this, alternate between trying to keep your finger as near the table as you can while still tapping and letting your finger come up a good*

*distance off the table. You probably will find it hard to produce a big speed difference. You may also notice that it is difficult to keep your finger near the table when you are tapping really fast.*

Proponents of trigger slapping have their own case to make. One of the main arguments in favor of this technique is that shooters feel that it eliminates the possibility of "trigger freeze." Trigger freeze is usually described as what happens when a shooter doesn't let the trigger far enough out to reset between shots. This causes a noticeable pause in their shooting. It stands to reason that if the trigger is intentionally released much further than the reset point, then it wouldn't be possible to "trigger freeze" (or so that argument goes). I don't think this argument really holds up. I have personally experienced a "trigger freeze" by not pushing the trigger hard enough or far enough to discharge the gun in the first place. It is a very similar phenomenon to what people commonly describe as "trigger freeze," and it can certainly happen when using the slapping method.

Arguments about these things are pretty much all that separate the various schools of thought. There are many other issues that people may point to, but they are just as insignificant as the other issues I discussed. The fact is that there are fantastic world-class shooters who use each of the methods described. After closely studying this issue for a great deal of time, it is tough to make an argument that it really makes a difference which school of thought someone subscribes to.

Right up front, I need to point to an issue that I skipped in the "Grip" section, because I think it fits better here. Finger placement on the trigger certainly is an issue and needs to be addressed. Most competitors shooting the sort of guns that are used for USPSA will prefer to have the pad of their trigger finger on the trigger most of the time. It is important to pay attention to the precise placement of your pad to try to pull the trigger straight back. Small adjustments can make things a lot easier for you. Every hand is different, and there are many types of guns out there. That is why there needs to be some experimentation on your part to find out the exact trigger finger placement that makes things easiest for you.

Another consideration that shooters with heavy triggers, or perhaps double action triggers, may have is that under certain circumstances (like shooting with only one-hand) they may want to try moving their finger placement all the way to the first joint. This will provide a lot of leverage and allow that person to better press the trigger. When it comes to trigger finger placement, experimentation is important.

Before I can get into how to best control the trigger, I need to address one thing that will come up a lot over the next few pages, and that thing is "trigger prep." Trigger prep is the ability to manipulate the trigger right up until the point just before the gun will discharge. This is done because most people who use this technique find it easier to carefully pull the trigger when they only need to do so for a small portion of the trigger's total travel. Let me explain why it doesn't really matter.

To refresh your memory, here are the two marksmanship fundamentals:

1.  Align the muzzle of the gun with the target.
2.  Hold that alignment until you discharge the firearm.

Trigger control falls under the second fundamental. We need to hold the alignment of the firearm while the trigger is manipulated. More precisely, we need to pull the trigger without disturbing the sights any more than the difficulty of the shot we are undertaking allows us to. What this means in practical terms is that to hit the "A" zone of a close range target, we can disturb the sight alignment a great deal and still hit the "A" zone. At longer ranges, we need to pull the trigger in such a way that we disturb that alignment much less.

All of the trigger techniques that I described absolutely meet the fundamental requirements. If you practice one of them, you will be able to shoot fast and accurately. The truth is that what matters is breaking the shot without disturbing the sights. All the other things that people argue about in terms of trigger technique don't really have anything to do with the actual instant that the gun is being fired. It really shouldn't matter whether your finger comes off the trigger or you hold the trigger back, because in that actual instant you aren't firing. The disagreement over trigger control technique essentially boils down to much ado about nothing.

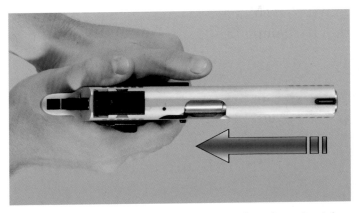

*Pull the trigger straight to the rear without disturbing the sights.*

There are some important practical considerations, however.

Most guns have a very particular trigger "feel." A Glock feels one way. The trigger breaks at a certain point and needs to be released a certain distance to reset. If the gun is modified, then these properties change. No two guns really feel identical. This can become an issue for people that utilize the "pin and reset" technique. If someone learns one particular gun, and then switches platforms, they can have trouble learning to shoot the new gun. Since they want to let the trigger out just to the point of reset they often need a bit of retraining to "learn the reset" on an unfamiliar platform. With the trigger slapping technique, this is not really an issue.

Another issue is having a trigger technique that works for guns that have more than one trigger pull. Double action guns like CZs and Sigs require the shooter to learn how to use two distinct trigger pulls. It may be easier for someone learning these platforms to adopt a trigger technique that allows them to easily use both trigger modes.

## From Matthew Mink (IDPA National Champion, IPSC National Champion, IPSC World Shoot Gold Medalist)

### Trigger Speed

*Trigger speed is a topic that should interest almost all shooters, because so many new shooters get hung up on how fast they can "split." I think this is a skill that is tough to teach, because some have it and some don't. I don't think it is the final answer to winning matches, but it is a way I can shave some time here and there in a match. Obviously the more "hoser" targets there are, the more ground you can gain. The opposite is also true. With fewer wide-open targets present, there is not as much opportunity to utilize trigger speed.*

*I developed trigger speed over many years. There are some drills you should do that are obvious, like the Bill Drill. I have also found that you have to stay completely relaxed, no tension anywhere. Also, if I am over thinking it, it won't happen. I have to just roll up and execute it.*

*Matthew Mink with two pieces of brass in the air.*

*On really close targets where I can get rolling, .10 to .12 splits aren't uncommon with my Production gear, resulting in all "A"s with startling regularity. I was told long ago that I shouldn't do that because it was "dangerous." Since this person was a former World and National champion, I listened. I have since realized that what he meant was, he could not shoot splits and hit "A"s that fast, so I shouldn't either, so he could keep winning. I went back to believing in myself and shooting the way I wanted to. My game got better, and I think there is a lesson in that.*

It should be clear at this point that it doesn't make sense to slavishly adhere to a particular school of thought as far as trigger control goes. Don't worry so much if you know your trigger finger is hopping off the trigger a little bit on close-range targets. Don't think that there is some technical magic concept that is going to make the trigger go straight back to the rear on its own. Trigger control is a challenging thing to learn, and it isn't helpful to saddle yourself with a bunch of dogma along the road.

The solution to this whole trigger control issue is to learn a few different methods that work based upon the circumstance. For long distance targets pull the trigger one way, for close targets pull it another, and in the middle pull the trigger some other way.

This may sound complicated, and it is, but without more than one trigger control technique it is going to be difficult to be fast when you need to be fast, and be accurate when you need to be accurate. Some people may think that since either "slapping" or "pinning" both work, we could just use one of those techniques. In truth, each one of those schools of thought involves learning to pull the trigger a different way depending on the difficulty of the shot. You are going to end up in the same place, eventually, no matter what route you take.

In the training book *Champion Shooting: A Proven Process for Success at any Level* Jay Hirshberg laid out a plan with three types of trigger control. This bears repeating here:

Trigger control comes in three general styles:

Type 1: You are not setting the trigger to the break point, you're just blasting through the shot, noting the sights, lifting and moving to the next shot. This type is used for close-up targets where you pull straight through the trigger.

Type 2: Set the trigger to the break point and pull through that point with reasonable speed. This type is used for a mid-length shot or a shot requiring a degree of accuracy.

Type 3: A clearly defined set to the trigger break point and a pull-through while maintaining clear discipline on the sights. Ensure that you have no movement of the sight plane of the gun. This type is used for the highest degree of accuracy, like a 30-yard popper.

These aren't the only possible types or the only valid types, but if you look at it in terms of having a system for dealing with any type of shot you will encounter, this is at least a workable plan. Use this system, or perhaps develop one of your own, using the ideas available in this chapter.

I think it is fair to say that most shooters will naturally work themselves into a system where they have a whole continuum of possible types of trigger control. It just depends on how difficult the shot is.

My own trigger control development was intuitive. First, I learned how to fire an accurate shot. The only thing I cared about was pressing the trigger straight back. After being able to shoot an accurate shot, I was just less and less careful about the "quality" of the trigger press as I started shooting faster. I learned how careful I needed to be for any given difficulty of shot. The less careful I needed to be, the faster I could go. The reason I don't come down on this trigger control discussion with a firm recommendation is that any of the techniques I listed can get you where you want to go. The most important element is learning to fire a really accurate shot. Once you have that ability, you can learn to be less careful with your trigger control when the targets are closer and easier.

# THE DRAW

The draw (or presentation, if you prefer that term) is something that USPSA shooters are going to do a lot of. Most stages start with the gun in your holster. You need to learn to quickly and consistently get the gun out of the holster, in a firm consistent grip, and pointed at a target (assuming you have one to shoot).

I do want to take a little time to address why the draw is so important. I will admit drawing isn't a huge part of your time on most stages. If you think about it, drawing is just a small percentage of your time on a 20-second stage. For this reason, I think many people rationalize being slow at it. This is a really big mistake. Draw speed is strongly correlated with how fast you are at shooting generally. It makes sense if you think about it. You look to a target, grip your pistol (hopefully in a consistent fashion), then point the gun to the target. This is just a more complicated version of a regular target transition. Transitions are something you do a lot of on most stages. For this reason, if you are fast at drawing, you are usually fast at transitioning. If you are fast at transitioning, then you are fast at shooting stages. So, you should get fast at drawing.

We should start with the most commonly taught and utilized draw technique in USPSA. Most shooters use this exact technique or some slight variation of it.

1. When the shooter is given the start signal, they immediately acquire a firing grip on the pistol with their dominant hand while the pistol is still in the holster.

2. While the dominant hand is getting a grip on the pistol, the non-dominant hand moves over very near to the front of the holster. The hand can't be in a position where the gun will be pointed at it at any time after the gun clears the holster, but getting your non-dominant very near to that point is helpful.

3. As soon as a firing grip is obtained with the dominant hand, the gun is pulled from the holster and moved up toward the shooter's normal firing position. During this time, the non-dominant hand acquires a firing grip on the pistol.

4. Once the gun is up at eye level, the shooter aims to the extent necessary for the target they are shooting and breaks the shot when they are ready. This is exactly the same idea that is presented in great detail in the "Target Transition" section and why the draw can be thought of as "just another transition."

I think the above elements are fairly uncontroversial as far as USPSA shooters go. If you want to get an idea of how this draw feels, you can do the following exercise. Stand normally, as if you are shooting a target (aim at it and everything). While standing like that, reholster the gun slowly. Move the gun back in toward your body, then back down toward the holster. When the gun is near the holster, take your non-dominant hand off the gun, then reholster. This may sound like a silly exercise, but if you give it a chance, you will get a good idea of how an efficient draw "feels."

Now, the problem with drawing the pistol from the holster isn't really about accomplishing the essential elements. Even the most novice shooter will be able to take the gun from the holster, get a grip on it, and fire at a target. The problem is doing the steps I described and only those steps in an expeditious manner.

There are all kinds of things people do during the draw process that are unnecessary and waste time. I will explain those things quickly so you can get an idea of the common problems people have.

The first problem I commonly see is a slow reaction to the start signal. When a shooter hears the start signal, it is important that they respond immediately and aggressively to the first note of the buzzer. The first thing that needs to be done is to obtain a firing grip on the gun, and there is no reason for any delay. One good little drill to try to correct this issue is to attach a shot timer to your holster instead of your gun. With the timer in the same position as your holster, you can respond to the start signal simply by slapping the timer. The timer should record this as a shot.

Then you can work to reduce that time. This should give you a good sensation of moving your arms very aggressively. (This exercise works even better when utilizing a "wrists above the shoulders" start position.)

Another extremely common issue is for a shooter to push down on their gun hard when they are getting a grip on it. You can see this happen with many people. Their belt will flex and the holster will visibly move down an inch or two while they are gripping the gun. This obviously adds a bit of time to the draw. It is faster to simply get a proper grip and snatch the gun from the holster. It shouldn't be necessary to grind the gun into the holster in order to get a grip. Pay attention to the feeling of the gun on your hip if you suspect this may be an issue you have. If you feel yourself pushing down on the gun, work to correct it.

Many shooters don't get their non-dominant hand over to the holster. This isn't an issue and doesn't cause problems for most people unless they start trying to go really fast. When a shooter is pushing the draw hard, their non-dominant hand will often end up "chasing" the gun out toward the target. This is why it is good practice early on in a shooter's training and development to get that hand over toward the holster as soon as possible. Upper level shooters should pay attention to this as well.

Another issue I frequently see is a person moving their body around during the first part of the draw (the getting to the gun part). People tend to lean away from the gun, crouch down, or do any number of things. It is important to minimize motion. Generally speaking, if you are moving something other than your arms during the draw, you want to stop moving that thing. There are exceptions to this of course. For example, some larger (girth-wise) shooters may have a problem getting their hand on the gun if they don't lean away from the holster. When moving really fast, it is very difficult to entirely eliminate twisting your hips. If you have some sort of issue like that, just do the best you can. Pay attention during your training to every little motion you make, and be certain it is something that you need to be doing. If in doubt, think back to the "reverse draw" exercise I outlined earlier. You can always do things slowly in reverse to be certain of the motion you need to be making and to see if you are making a motion you don't want to be making. You could also try practicing in front of a full-length mirror.

If extraneous motion is a problem for you, there is another exercise you can try. Put your back against a pole or a small tree, and then practice drawing. If there is any motion other than in your arms, you will be able to feel it. This little drill has helped me a great deal.

Once the gun clears the holster, the most common issue is for the gun to take an inefficient path toward the target. The gun should move in a more or less straight line from the holster to the target. Going over the target and bringing the gun back down is commonly called "fishing." It is a common issue. Along those same lines, extending the arms all the way out to their eventual firing position, then moving the gun up toward the target is inefficient (that is called "bowling"). The gun needs to move more or less in a straight line toward its firing position.

An easy test for an efficient draw path is to pay very careful attention to the sight picture and the gun when you draw. Ideally, you will see the sights come up in alignment and settle in to the center of your target. If you see the front sight come up high, then drop down onto the target, that is a good indication of fishing.

There is some disagreement in the shooting community as to the exact path the gun needs to take from the holster up to the firing position. Some shooters prefer an absolutely straight line while others prefer to get the sights up to the eye line as quickly as possible. The rationale for the latter technique is that if the sights are between the eyes and the target, the shooter can begin aiming before the draw is complete. In some older USPSA texts (such as Brian Enos' fantastic book and Plaxco's also pretty good book) you will find instructions for constructing a "trainer" device out of PVC pipe or a piece of string. This device can essentially train you to keep the gun closer to your chest as you draw it from the holster and move it up toward the firing position. The effect of training with this device would be to instill the technique of getting the gun to your eye line as soon as possible. If you are curious about constructing a training device like that, you should consult the relevant text in those books. Use of those devices has fallen out of favor in recent years with more shooters preferring the more "natural" draw path of the gun, getting up into the eye line only slightly before it is in position for firing.

## The Press-Out

There is a school of thought that says shooters should adopt a draw technique called the "press-out." Depending on whom you ask, the press-out technique has more than one definition. Many people believe that the press-out is simply bringing the gun all the way up to your face (I have even heard someone say that you should feel your rear sight rub on your cheek) and then "pressing out" toward the target while you aim. This is an exaggerated variation of the "old school" draw path that Enos and Plaxco seemed to be advocating.

Other people contend that the press-out technique should involve more than that. These people believe that the shooter should press the gun out more slowly or quickly depending on the difficulty of the target being engaged. The harder the target, the slower the press should be. The idea behind this is to work the trigger, aim, and draw all at the same time. If this is properly done, the shot will break just as the shooter reaches their regular firing position. A good way to conceptualize this is to imagine a piece of string attached to the shooter's shirt and tied around the trigger. The shooter presses the gun out and when the string gets tight, the gun goes off.

The press-out technique, described this way, is complicated. There is an adamant belief among many that this is the fastest and most accurate technique available. I will submit to you that no top competitive action shooter that I am aware of uses this rather complicated technique. The claim that this technique is faster or more accurate simply isn't borne out by any evidence.

The key argument in favor of this technique is that you start aiming sooner. It is self-evidently true that the *sooner you aim, the sooner you are able to fire. While it is true that the sooner you aim the better, it is not true that you aim appreciably sooner utilizing a press-out. It doesn't take more time to get the gun into firing position than it does to get the gun up to your eye line. The reason it doesn't is that your arms bring the gun up and push it out at the same time. The press-out technique is that you bring the gun up and then press it out. The conventional draw combines those two things (in an intuitive fashion) into one motion.*

Another very common mistake I see is a shooter grossly "over aiming" or "under aiming" at whatever target they are drawing to. It seems that many people have a tendency to aim much longer and harder than necessary at close-range, easy targets. It is up to individuals to discover for themselves the necessary level of aiming, but many people spend a few too many tenths of a second aiming most of the time. For example, on a seven-yard target, there shouldn't be much aiming required. Even with grossly mis-aligned sights it is still possible to get "A" zone hits. The opposite of "over aiming" is also true of many shooters. When some people decide they are going to "go fast," they simply throw the gun out in front of their face and start shooting. It is important to aim, even when the range is minimal. The target needs to be very close before no visual confirmation of sight alignment is necessary to ensure a hit. I am going to address this topic in depth in the "Target Transition" section, but know up front that this is a very common issue for shooters to struggle with when they draw the gun out of the holster.

The final common issue I will address is that of "slowing down" the draw when the shot is difficult. It really doesn't matter if the target is at 5 yards or 50 yards, the actual draw should be the same speed. Extra time will be added, but that will be aiming at the longer target, not actually changing the draw speed. It is extremely natural for a shooter to take their time when drawing to a target they judge as difficult. This is a mistake.

With the draw technique covered in depth at this point, it is a good idea to have a practical way to conceptualize the technique that will work in all circumstances (not just hands at sides, facing a target). Here is the method I recommend:

Step 1: Move your hands to the gun. Get a firing grip on the pistol with your dominant hand and have your non-dominant hand as near to the gun as you can safely get it, ready to receive the gun once it gets out of the holster.

Step 2: End up in a firing position, aimed at the target, ready to break the shot.

After you execute "Step 1," you move your body however you need to so you are in a position for "Step 2." This process is versatile!

I strongly prefer this simple two-step method to the four or six-step thing that I see many people are taught in tactical training schools and elsewhere. I think it is easier to evolve into a more advanced and developed style of draw if you keep things simple right from the get-go.

### The Scoop Draw

*Before I leave the draw technique behind, we need to talk about one final technique, the "scoop" draw. The scoop draw is a process that has been floating around for a while. It is widely regarded as the fastest draw technique that is viable for practical shooting, but it has some serious drawbacks.*

*The scoop draw essentially cuts the "get a firing grip on the gun" part of the process out of the conventional draw technique. Instead of getting a firing grip on the gun while it is holstered, the shooter comes from underneath the gun and "scoops" it from the holster in one smooth motion. The dominant hand grip gets fixed on the way out to engage the target. This type of technique is far more easily accomplished with a holster that has a flat surface the shooter can use to guide their hand toward the grip of the pistol.*

*It is probably evident at this point why this technique is not more popular. It is a good way to get disqualified for a dropped gun, even though it is a tenth or two faster than the conventional technique. For this reason, I don't recommend using a scoop draw in USPSA. It just isn't worth the risk. There are some amazingly talented and well-trained shooters that have gotten themselves into trouble with a scoop draw just because they were looking for an extra tenth or two on a close target at a major match. In my opinion, it isn't worth the risk.*

*Most people who utilize a scoop draw do not do so in every circumstance. They learn a conventional technique and a scoop technique, then utilize a scoop when they feel it offers a real advantage.*

All this discussion of draws probably has you wondering . . . What is a "good" draw? You may read on the internet about people putting up .65 draws or some other very fast time. The fact is, the best Production shooters in the game sometimes break one second in a match. However, this is very scenario dependent. In practice, most Master or Grand Master level shooters can consistently get under a second on a seven-yard target. As the distance increases, the top shooters only require a few tenths of a second more to aim. Drawing to long-range targets is usually where the better shooters really get ahead.

If you look back over this section, you will see that the draw is more about what you don't do, rather than what you do. The essential elements of the draw are simply to get you to shooting the shots you need to shoot. It is counterproductive to take detours along the way. It may seem condescending to point out all the common errors that people make, but it has to be done. Eliminate the wasted motion!

# INDEX

This is a good time to discuss "index." What I mean by "index" is probably different from some definition you may use. When I use index, I am talking about the speed at which you can line up your shooting platform with any given target. This is indicative of having a developed and robust draw, to the point where you can look to any given target, draw the gun, and have the sights come on to the target aligned and ready to shoot.

You may remember in "The Draw" section I mentioned that I think a fast draw and fast stage times are strongly correlated. I think this is the reason why. Once you have developed your index to a high level, then you should be correspondingly fast with target acquisition and shooting.

From an instructional standpoint, I would say I usually have a few guys in any given fundamentals class that do not have a very well developed index, usually due to a lack of regular dry-fire training. Normally, these guys can execute good trigger control, good recoil control, and a fast draw, but putting it all together at the same time is really tough for them. When they draw the gun, the sights aren't usually coming up in alignment (does this sound familiar?). I see them fighting with the gun when they transition from target to target. They are fighting to line up the sights every single time they transition. This is what you see when someone hasn't developed an index.

On the other hand, I see quite a few students that regularly dry-fire and have developed a really nice index. Anywhere they look, the gun follows, and the sights show up more or less aligned. Since these guys already have a developed index, I am able to push their shooting speed much further, much faster.

There are a few things you can do to test your index if you aren't sure whether it is any good. The easiest test is to stand facing forward, with targets all over the place in the 180-degree arc in front of you. Simply look at any target, draw the gun and make sure the sights come up in alignment on that target.

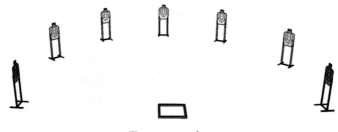

*Test your index.*

Another good test is to close your eyes, then draw your gun. Open your eyes. If you have the gun in front of you at eye level with the sights lined up, you probably have a pretty well developed index.

I imagine there are two kinds of people reading this. Those that are like "Yeah, duh," and those that don't experience their shooting this way. If you are in the latter group, then you need to start training to get your index developed. I don't think you need to work on specific drills to develop your index, just start working a variety of drills, and eventually you will not have to fight to see the sights any longer. They will just go where you look and more or less be in alignment.

## From Bob Vogel (IDPA World Champion, IPSC World Champion)

### *Draw and Grip*
*Having a hard grip on the gun is really important to me. On a big stage, though, the actual draw time doesn't mean*

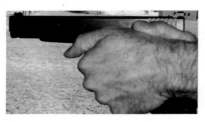

*Bob Vogel demonstrating his grip.*

*very much. That is why I spend an extra tenth of a second during the draw to really bear down on my grip. When I draw, it looks like I have a "hitch." The "hitch" is just me grinding my hands into the gun and gripping down as hard as I can. I don't bother with this on close targets.*

*Bob Vogel.*

# STANCE

Stance is one of those things that I think most people pay a lot of attention to for the wrong reasons. I want to make it obvious right away where I am going with this, so I will just make it as plain as possible. Stance doesn't have a whole lot to do with recoil control. Yes, I know we have all seen YouTube videos of some girl shooting a Desert Eagle while she is leaning backward. Obviously, her stance is really messed up and that is a bad thing. Aside from making a really egregious error like that, I think the primary consideration you need to be thinking about when it comes to stance is mobility.

Before I get too far down the road of discussing shooting stance, I want to give a proper definition of exactly what it is I am talking about. For our

*This is enough forward weight bias.*

purposes, "stance" will be your body position from your feet up to your arms. From the arms up, we will worry about that separately.

With the definition stuff out of the way, let's talk about the three things that we are going to be concerned with when it comes to stance. These things are listed in order of importance.

1.  Mobility
2.  Stability
3.  Comfort

First, it is important to understand that USPSA is an extremely dynamic sport. On longer courses of fire, the shooter will spend most of their time moving, setting up in a new position, or leaving a position they just shot from. There really isn't all that much truly "static" shooting in the sport. We run around all the time. It is probably intuitively clear to people that we need a shooting stance that allows us to be mobile.

At the same time as we want to be mobile, we need to be stable. USPSA shooters are often engaging targets while moving through a stage or while getting into a position. If we have a stance that gives us a stable shooting platform during these times, we will clearly have an advantage.

Finally, it is important to remain comfortable to some degree. Contorting yourself into a position that is perhaps marginally more effective than a more comfortable or natural position doesn't strike most USPSA shooters as a very good trade-off. Not many people are very enthusiastic about spending long hours doing dry-fire or training on the range if they are going to end up irritated and sore as a result.

With these three primary goals in mind, I am going to describe the "state of the art" USPSA stance. Most top USPSA shooters seem to have a very similar stance as they move through a course of fire. I am going to describe the elements, highlight a few interesting differences, then discuss a few other options.

It is widely agreed upon in USPSA circles that the best way to shoot is with your body more or less square to the target that you are engaging. This would preclude an older technique like the "Weaver Stance." The reasoning behind standing squarely facing the target is that the stance is "neutral." By standing squarely, the shooter isn't favoring one side or the other and is able to get to the next target quickly, no matter where it may be.

In terms of foot position, shooters generally stand with their feet a little bit wider than shoulder width apart. For comfort's sake, most people put their holster side foot a few inches behind their other foot. This is a good position to get moving from. It allows you to push off with your feet and get going toward the next position you need to go to.

The knees need to be bent. This is a critical element when you start moving around. Properly bent knees act as "shock absorbers." The idea here is that you can move over the shooting range (often rough terrain) and still maintain a stable sight picture by using your knees in this fashion.

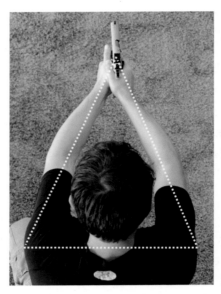

*Notice there is an "upper body triangle."*

Moving up to the arms, shooters form a triangle (more or less) with their arm position. They simply grip the gun and hold it out in front of their face. Viewed from the top, this looks like a triangle. Viewed from the sides, your non-dominant arm is going to sit slightly higher. This is because you can get that hand higher up on the gun, so the arm will end up correspondingly higher. In terms of having an "aggressive stance" or leaning forward, the upper echelon shooters stand more or less vertically, with a slight forward weight bias. This seems to fly in the face of advice that non-competitive shooting instructors often give in which people are often advised to "lean into" the gun to a much more serious extent. If you are leaning into the gun just a little, the gun will not push you backward when you are firing it at high speed. As long as you aren't getting pushed over, it doesn't help to lean even more forward.

With the fundamentals and the top shooter's technique on the table, we can move forward with this information and shape it into a useful conceptual understanding.

It is helpful to think of stance as a series of guidelines that should be applied to every shooting situation and position instead of as a specific technique to be executed. I can enumerate the guidelines below so you get an idea of what I am talking about.

1. Keep your knees bent.
2. Have a slight forward weight bias (shoulders in front of hips is a good guideline).
3. Stand squarely facing targets. It is helpful to imagine a line on the ground going straight out from your foot. The line should go directly away from your big toe. If you have a line going from each foot, it will form a cone in front of you. It is helpful to keep any targets you are engaging in the cone.

I call these things guidelines because they are merely that. These are not hard and fast rules. Good shooting can still be done when these guidelines are violated, but in terms of a best practice, it is useful to try to work within these guidelines, if possible. I can explain them more fully now.

**Guideline 1:** Keep your knees bent. If you are able to maintain bent knees, you will get the "shock absorber" effect that I discussed earlier. This is only important if you are moving. It works really well, but you need to be careful how you train yourself to do it. It is extremely common for people to "get low" when shooting on-the-move, and then stand up when they stop to shoot from a static position. Standing back up fully erect after getting down lower will cost you time. It is a good idea to always be on guard against standing back up again after you get low.

**Guideline 2:** Keep your shoulders in front of your hips. If you have a slight forward lean at all times, you should have enough weight into the gun to keep it from pushing you around. This applies at all times. If you are kneeling down or leaning around a wall, it applies. No matter what the specific circumstance is, it is useful to have that forward weight bias. If you are unable to keep a little bit of weight forward (due to the specifics of the stage), you may need to slow your rate of fire to keep the gun from rocking you totally off balance.

*It is best to engage targets in this "cone" area. The more difficult the shot required, the more helpful it is to be squarely facing that target.*

**Guideline 3:** Stand square to the targets. The more difficult the shot is, the more essential it is to stand squarely facing the targets. The reason for this will be obvious if you undertake the following exercise. Stand in a normal stance with your gun pointed straight downrange. If you twist your body left or right far enough, you will feel some tension in your shoulders. This tension in the shoulders can make it tough to make tight shots at any sort of speed. It shouldn't matter on easy targets, but if it is a target that would be hard to hit under normal circumstances just standing there, it is helpful to be square to the target.

The practical effect of all this stance stuff is interesting. In a practical shooting class setting for example, I very rarely need to even make mention of anything stance related when doing static drills on a firing line. People intuitively and naturally seem to understand the things that I just explained. It is very rare that someone will be shooting without a forward weight bias. I can't recall ever seeing anyone shoot without being more or less squared up to the targets. Keeping the knees bent is irrelevant when shooting static.

The interesting thing about all this is that as soon as the drills become dynamic movement–based drills, these guidelines are violated with regularity, and it has a very negative impact on people's shooting. A common example of this is people getting into position to lean around a wall. It is extremely common for someone who naturally sets up to shoot a single target during static drills from a proper stance to really make a mess of things when they set up to lean around a wall. The lesson here is that people generally need to learn to apply stance guidelines on actual stages, not standing and punching holes in cardboard.

One interesting topic that requires a close look is that of arm and elbow position. This is one area where you do see quite a bit of variation among upper level shooters. This variation is likely not terribly consequential, but it is there, and it makes sense to try to understand it.

It seems intuitive and natural for people to think that if they push out with their arms as far as they can, even to the point of hyperextending the elbows, then they will somehow gain more control over the gun. This isn't demonstrably true as far as I can tell. Even if this were true, many people hold the gun out in front of themselves (without locking the elbows) and are able to control the gun while shooting as fast as they can pull the trigger. More recoil control than this (even if possible) doesn't seem like it would have any effect at all on your shooting.

What most top-level shooters do (for comfort's sake) is to have a fairly significant bend to the elbows. This brings the gun an inch or two in closer to the face and for most people feels a lot more comfortable. Some shooters bend the elbows out, and some bend them down. The effect on recoil control for any of these options doesn't seem consequential.

It is commonly asserted by many shooting instructors that "rolling the shoulders forward" will produce better recoil control. I have tested this method extensively and have never been able to show that this is the case. In any event, the argument about hyperextended elbows just above would still apply. It isn't worth sacrificing comfort for a marginal and undetectable amount of recoil control, especially when you consider that the techniques already discussed offer enough recoil control to run a pistol as fast as your trigger finger will allow.

Another issue that needs to be discussed before we leave stance behind is the effect it has on target transitions. Most upper level shooters, especially Steel Challenge competitors, use their legs heavily during target transitions. This isn't an issue when the targets are very close together, but with widely spaced targets it can be. Some shooters talk about "getting their legs into it" or maybe even about feeling the target transitions start in their toes. It does offer a speed advantage to use your legs to help transition between targets more aggressively.

The reason that this is being brought up in this section is that it obviously won't work if your legs are not in a position to help push your body. This means that to gain a transition speed advantage, your feet both need to be planted firmly on the ground and be spread a bit wider than shoulder length apart. You won't have much leverage to "push" your body if you don't do this. This was explained outside of the normal stance guidelines because it is not a dynamic technique. This can only work when standing still.

Finally, understand that how your body is set up in a given position will affect how easy it is to leave that position. Having a foot in a good spot to push you out of position is something to consider. There will be more on these sorts of issues in the "Stage Breakdown" section.

# TARGET TRANSITIONS

Target transitions are the area where most mid-level shooters lose the most time in a match situation. If you are currently a "pretty good" shooter, maybe A or B class, then this is probably the lowest hanging fruit for you. You can make the biggest gains with the least amount of effort. It is important to get that out right up front to make sure that people pay very close attention to this section.

Before I get too deep into transitions, I want to be clear that the way I am discussing transitions in this book is only target transitions. Some shooters (especially our IPSC friends from outside the United States) will use the term "transition" to include moving from one shooting position to another. I will address that separately later in the book.

Fundamentally, a target transition is to align the gun with the next target, then hold it there until the shot breaks. As usual I can break it down into more complicated steps.

1. Find the target with your eyes.
2. Bring the gun to the spot you are looking at.
3. Refine the sight picture as necessary.
4. Keep the gun on your "spot" until you are done shooting the target.

Let's start at the beginning. The first thing you need to do is locate the next target you plan to shoot. Obviously, you are going to need to find the target in your vision, because that is where you are going to direct the gun to. However, I want to be really specific about how you should define "target" in this instance. I don't mean the big brown thing; I mean you should look to the exact spot you want to hit. The center of the "A" zone. The center of the calibration circle on a popper. If you are dealing with a partial target, then you should have picked an exact aiming point (this will be covered in a later section).

I don't want to belabor the point here, but I really want to emphasize that the gun is going to go exactly where you end up looking. This happens for better or worse. I frequently see students that are sloppy about picking an aim point on a target who give up a huge number of points for no good reason. Either people look to the wrong spot on a close easy target and give up points, or they end up just shooting at brown. Please don't neglect this step. Find the center. Find the spot you want to hit.

Let's move on to the "bring the gun to the spot" part. Most shooters are instructed early on in their shooting career to move their eyes to the next target, and then let the gun follow. This might seem counterintuitive to some people. Some shooters are naturally inclined to focus on the sight picture while looking down the sights, and then move that sight picture to the next place it needs to be without losing focus on it.

*Find the target with your eyes, and then bring the gun to the spot.*

It can be demonstrated pretty easily why this is prob-lematic just by using a computer. Try to move a mouse pointer around on the screen while never taking your eye off the mouse pointer. Keep that mouse pointer the center of your attention. You will almost certainly find it impos-sible to move it quickly from spot to spot on the screen while maintaining focus on it. If you try moving your eyes to where you want the pointer to show up, and then bring the pointer into your vision, you will easily be able to click on anything you like. You should use your sights just like that mouse pointer! Look where you want to go, and then bring the sights to the spot.

When teaching classes, I will often ask a student why they think they shot a couple "C" hits on a close range target. They will often say "trigger control" or "flinch" when I saw them simply aim in the wrong spot on the tar-get. You always need to get your eyes to exactly where you want to hit!

You need to build a certain degree of consistency in your technique before your sights will behave like a mouse pointer. Again, this is where your "index" will come in to play. If you don't have an index, then you are going to be unable to develop high-speed target transitions.

### Post in the Notch

*One concept that has helped me a great deal is to try to keep the front sight post centered in the notch while I transition. I don't mean that you should look at the sights while you transition; you shouldn't. However, you should see the sights come onto the next target and already be lined up when they get there. If they aren't lined up, you probably changed your upper body position or grip during the transition. This is a big help, especially on relatively wide target transitions.*

When you transition to the next target, you want the gun to move smoothly to the target. You don't want to see the gun come to a "jerky" stop on the target (with the muzzle of the gun momentarily shaking). Ideally, the gun snaps from one target to the next, moving with precision from one aiming zone to the next.

I think that initially during your training, you want to "muscle" the gun as little as possible. Simply look where you want to go and let the gun go to that spot. Focus on efficiency and precision and don't worry too much about speed. Think about the mouse pointer again. When you want to click on something on your screen really fast, you don't consciously slam the mouse around as hard as you can. No, you just look where you want to go and precisely bring the mouse to that spot.

The ideal sensation is to look at a spot and have the gun and sights settle right on that spot. If you see the sights go past your desired aim point, then return to the aim point, you "overswung" the transition. You pushed the gun too hard.

Of course, you want to transition as fast as possible, and eventually you will be doing transitions that are a bit wider and perhaps require more effort to quickly move the gun. This ends up being a bit of a balancing act. Any force or muscle you put in to the gun must be careful and calculated. Work hard to avoid "overswinging."

Guys at the highest levels of the sport are even able to use their feet to help them push the gun faster from one target to the next. Generally, this is going to be done on wider (at least 45-degree) transitions. Using your muscles should be carefully calculated and controlled. It isn't about pushing the gun hard; it is about pushing it precisely.

This is a good spot to reiterate something from the "Grip" section. You hold the gun with your hands. So often people use arm and shoulder tension to try to control the gun. That works all right on one target, but it is too much work to do that stuff and still transition the gun around quickly. If you are struggling with transition precision, then check your shoulders for tension. It could be the cause of your problems.

After you get the gun movement part down, then the next step in a target transition is aiming to the degree necessary for whatever target you are shooting. This is an extremely complicated issue. Every shooter has a different sight setup, skill level, and so forth. Also, the variety of targets and target distances encountered in USPSA makes things even more complicated. Aiming could mean just seeing a flash of a fiber optic sight in the center of a close target, or it could mean seeing a really sharp front sight blade settled and stable on a target.

Below, I have a non-inclusive list of aiming options.

1. Having your arms aligned with the target.
2. Pointing the gun at the target (aiming done by tactile feel).
3. Seeing an outline of your gun on the target.
4. Seeing a fiber optic dot on the target while your vision is focused on the target.
5. Seeing a blurry sight picture on the target while your vision is focused on the target.
6. Having an optical focus on the front sight while your sights are on target.
7. Having an optical focus on the front sight and making sure that the sight is "settled" into the target.
8. Having an optical focus on the front sight and making sure that the sight is "settled" into the target, and the front and rear blade are in equal height/equal light alignment.
9. Having a stable, front sight focused sight picture with equal height/equal light alignment, then holding that picture while the trigger is carefully manipulated.

This list, while not inclusive of every possible way to aim at a target, is a pretty good start. You might look at some of them and think that they hardly even qualify as aiming. Pointing the gun at a target with no visual reference (Number 2) isn't something that you do a whole lot of in USPSA, but it is certainly something that I have had to do. Along those same lines, you don't very often do (Number 9), but it is certainly something you may need to do when shooting at a 30-yard mini popper or some other similarly difficult target.

You need to engage your brain for USPSA. You need to think about what you can get away with. You need to experiment for yourself and find out the absolute minimum amount of aiming you can do and still get decent hits. To help you along, let me give you a couple guidelines that I personally use.

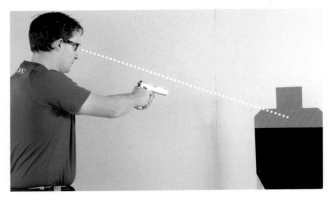

*Immediately shoot when the gun "breaks" the line.*

If the target is seven yards or closer, there shouldn't be a pause between when the gun comes in to your vision and the shot breaks. Draw a line between your eye and the target. When your gun breaks that line, you should immediately be shooting. There isn't a need for a pause while you refine the sight picture or pull your vision back on to the front sight blade. You should be aligned enough that you are able to shoot.

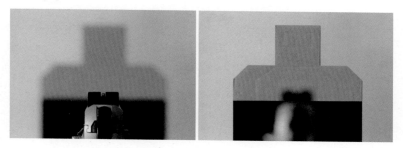

*Examples of front sight focus and target focus on the same target.*

On the subject of focus on the target or on the front sight, I find that about 80 percent of the shots in USPSA are fired "target focused" by me. I am comfortable shooting to about 15 yards in a match setting on wide-open USPSA targets with just target focus.

Once you get the aiming method sorted out, the last step is to hold your aim on the spot until you are done shooting the target. This probably seems obvious to the point of being redundant and self-evident, but the fact is that this is a good way to pick up misses in match situations.

There are a couple common mistakes I want to point out when it comes to keeping your aim on a spot until you are done with it. When you start training yourself to transition very quickly, you will probably be tempted to start "sweeping" an array of targets. By this, I mean you will keep the gun moving the entire time. This isn't what you want. You want to train yourself to have the gun move precisely from one spot to the next and stop on each spot. Sweeping will lead to imprecise hits (at best) and more likely some misses. It just plain doesn't work to keep the gun moving the whole time, so if you catch yourself doing it, make yourself stop.

Probably the more common sort of mistake I make (and see other people make) is to move my eye off the target I am currently shooting, and look toward the next target. Remember what I said earlier, the gun goes where you look for better or worse. This is kind of like when you check the lane next to you on the highway and your car drifts toward that lane because you turn the wheel a bit. Your gun works the same way! You train yourself to aim where you look, so you need to be disciplined about where you are looking!

I think that looking to the next target, before you are done with the current target, usually manifests when you are rushing. You might mentally be done on a target. You located and aimed at it, then broke the first shot. Since the target is close and easy, the second shot will be fired without letting the sights settle again. Until the second shot actually breaks, you need to keep your eye on the target you are shooting! Watch carefully for "dragging" shots on and off target when you working on fast transitions.

Anyway, I want to talk about a few other issues that tend to come up in the transition discussion:

I think one topic that bears mentioning in relation to transitions is distance changeups. One of the toughest things to do in USPSA, from a technical shooting sense, is efficiently transitioning from targets of different distances and difficulties to completely different targets. Famous drills like "Distance Changeup" and "Accelerator" have drawn the interest of so many shooters precisely because they are so challenging.

You might have a hard time going from close range high-speed target focused shredding to long-range precise shooting. This is challenging because you need to switch from one set of mechanics to another set entirely and do it in the space of about a third of a second. Instead of shooting target focused as fast as you can pull the trigger, you switch in to shooting hard front sight focused with a very disciplined trigger press.

You might be similarly challenged when shooting long-range precise targets, then going to the close-up shredding. It isn't abnormal for people to be way too slow on the close targets. If you find yourself in this situation, it may be helpful to rewire your brain a bit. Instead of looking at a close range target and thinking "that target is easy," you might instead want to think "that target is fast," and treat it accordingly.

In case this isn't abundantly clear by this point, target transitions are an area that is technical and complicated, but the payoff for mastering these concepts is huge. I have a few concepts I want you to try in your own training. These ideas have helped me push students to the next level. If you are willing to work a bit, you can get yourself to the next level as well.

1. It is often helpful to give yourself a "push" when training to get between targets fast.
2. Be sure to mix in targets of different difficulty levels when training.
3. Experiment with different methods of aiming at different targets.

When I assert that it is helpful to give yourself a "push," I mean that you need to actively try to go just a bit faster than you are comfortable going, and then carefully observe the results. You can use a par time. You can shoot with someone faster, and then try to match the sound of their shooting with your own shooting. You could even shoot an array of targets, then separate the targets (so you have a wider transition), and then match the pace of your first run. All of these methods will give you a little push to be just a little bit quicker from target to target. Be careful with this though, as most people completely break down if they get pushed too hard. You don't want your technique to fall completely apart, you just want to strain a bit.

Pushing yourself a bit, while necessary, is also something you need to be careful about, especially with dry-fire training. In dry-fire, you aren't getting feedback on where your bullets would have hit, so you can easily train yourself to pull off targets early or to not sufficiently aim at a target. You especially need to be honest with yourself during your dry-fire training. You then need to validate this with some real live-fire training.

*One issue that often comes up when discussing target transitions is that of "cadence." Firing in "cadence" is firing shots in a certain predetermined rhythm. This can be an excellent training tool to help push you to the next level in terms of speed. Be warned, trying to force yourself to shoot in "cadence" in a match situation can lead to misses.*

The idea behind mixing in a bunch of different target difficulties in the same string of fire is also critical when training (Number 2). I mentioned this before, but it bears emphasis. This is one of the most common places people fall down during matches. I know it is convenient during your training to place targets at a common distance and work those targets for that day, but things don't usually look like that during major matches. You should be absolutely comfortable with radical changes in difficulty and tempo of your shooting.

Finally, don't be afraid to try different things with different targets. Try shooting with a "target focus" on 25-yard targets. Try shooting with a front sight focus on three-yard targets. Try all sorts of things. You might be really surprised how fast you can be one way or how accurate you can be some other way. There is no reason not to experiment during your training.

There is one thought I want to leave you with on target transitions. If you are stuck in the rut of trying to be fast and not getting faster, then you may want to focus instead on doing things immediately. Look to the next target, the gun comes over immediately. The instant you see an acceptable sight picture, you shoot. Then the instant you are done, you move to the next target. If ever you see the sights lined up on a target, and you aren't shooting, then you are wasting time. If you are done shooting a target and are busy looking at it and admiring the two little holes you just put in to it, then you are wasting time. Pay attention during your training for any wasted time and stamp it out.

# RELOADING

Getting a fresh magazine into the pistol is an important skill. For the Production and Single Stack shooters out there, you are going to do this more often than you draw the pistol out of a holster. Therefore, it is really important to get good at this. If this isn't something you can subconsciously do, then you need to work more at it.

Fundamentally, all that we are doing when we reload is replacing the magazine in the gun with a fresh one. Normally, this is done proactively on a USPSA stage. We generally reload between shooting positions in pre-planned locations. This isn't always the case. Sometimes people run out of ammunition without planning on it. This is colloquially known as the "Oh S***" reload. It is one of those things that shouldn't happen but frequently does anyway. I am going to discuss the typical reload first (the "speed" reload), and then cover what to do when out of ammunition (the "slide lock" (Oh S***) reload).

*Full speed reload.*

The commonly agreed upon process is to release the magazine in the gun with your dominant hand, and to simultaneously retrieve a magazine with your non-dominant hand. The fresh magazine is then inserted into the gun. At the conclusion of the reload, the shooter either continues moving to where they need to go in the stage, or they engage the next target depending on the specific scenario.

The commonly agreed upon process is one thing, but there are many little specifics that can help speed this process up or slow it down. There are also some little bones of contention that people have about reloading, and those need to be addressed. I want to address all this in great detail.

Let's take the reloading process in order. Before even discussing the mechanics of the reload, I want to point to one thing that people mess up constantly. Getting in a hurry to get the reload started, failing to aim the final shot just before the reload, and then picking up a miss on that target. Best practice on this is to make sure you are done shooting the shot preceding the reload before you actually start the reload. Don't break your grip, don't lower your arms, don't do anything. Finish the shooting part, and then start the reload.

Rule number one during a static reload is to immediately direct your attention to the gun. I relax this rule if I am moving around on a stage. However, if you aren't doing anything else (like running), then there is no reason not to direct your attention to the gun. This will tell you the status of your gun. It will help you confirm that the old magazine is clear and assist you in seating the fresh magazine. I frequently see students in a class setting not looking

*Look the magazine into the gun.*

at the gun when reloading, and I always wonder why. Looking at what you are doing with the gun is going to help.

Some shooters are skeptical of the "look the magazine into the gun" advice. It is true that many people are capable of reloading without looking, especially when they are just standing still on a practice range. The "look the magazine in" advice is for high-pressure USPSA events, not practice ranges. Things that are easy in practice become error prone in a match environment. It isn't that looking at the gun during the reload is faster, it is just one more thing to help you be consistent. There is no demonstrable speed advantage to looking at the next target when reloading, so it is important to put your eyes to work where they may actually help, and that is looking the reload into the gun.

In any event, once you come to the point of getting the old magazine out of the gun, you need to release that magazine somehow. Almost universally, people tend to do this with their dominant hand thumb. This is how most (good) guns are designed to be used, and it makes a lot of sense. Some shooters use their non-dominant thumb to press down on the magazine release. Some use a non-traditional magazine release like the HK style release on the trigger guard. Some shooters have a reversed mag release and use their trigger finger. There isn't a way to put this without coming off like a total jerk, but it needs to be said: If you are doing something other than the conventional way, you are probably doing it wrong. I have seen exactly two shooters over my entire shooting career do something other than the conventional technique of the dominant thumb pressing the mag release, and be what I would consider fast. Now, you may have too small hands and genuinely be unable to use your dominant thumb. You may be stuck shooting a gun with a different style release for one reason or another. I understand that. My point is this, stick with the conventional style of using your dominant thumb to release the magazine unless you just can't make it work.

Another issue that I should point to here is that of "flipping" the gun in your hand to help you reach the magazine release. Using this technique, you relax your dominant hand grip, and then move your hand around the gun so you can reach the magazine release button. I personally do this. I know of a few top shooters that do it. I shoot a Production-style gun and can't reach the magazine release with my thumb any other way. So long as you don't drop the gun when you do this (hasn't happened to me, has happened to other people), I think it is a perfectly safe technique.

The reason that I (and other people) shoot a gun that I need to "flip" to reach the magazine release should be pretty apparent in the "Grip" section. It is most important that the gun fit my hand in a shooting sense and being able to reach all the controls comes second. Flipping doesn't really cost any time, so I don't mind doing it.

If you are shooting a Limited- or Open-style gun where you can make any changes you want to the gun, you may still end up flipping the gun. A magazine release that protrudes enough for you to reach it without adjusting your grip may be so obnoxious that you inadvertently hit it just gripping the gun. You may also drop magazines out of the gun on table starts (because the gun pushes into the table). In any event, flipping the gun is something that many shooters are going to have to get comfortable doing due to the way guns (and hands) are designed.

Once you activate the magazine release, you should hold the gun as vertically as possible. You want gravity to assist you in clearing the spent magazine from the gun. Your attention being on the gun is also going to let you know when the old magazine is clear. If you are running around and not in a position to visually check if the magazine is clear of the gun, then you are going to need to rely on tactile feel to confirm that the magazine is clear. If you are running, generally you have a bit more time to make sure the magazine clears the gun. I like to punch the magazine button and hold the gun in "dump" position a fraction of a second longer than I think it needs, just to have the extra safety cushion.

*Steps of a reload.*

Once you get the magazine out of the gun, you need to get the gun positioned for the reload. It is easier for most shooters to bring the gun closer in toward their body. Generally speaking, bringing the gun closer and lower (roughly the top of your abdomen just below the pectoral muscles) is much more consistent. It is important to understand that while it is widely claimed that reloading "high" is the fastest in a practical setting (like moving around on a stage), this is not really demonstrably true for most Production guns. In fact, I will submit to you that the vast majority of shooters (regardless of what they train to do) drop the gun down low when reloading on the run. Having the gun a bit lower and closer gives you less "bounce" in the gun while you are running. I think for the sake of consistency, it makes sense to just accept this as a fact of life, and train to load in that position. There isn't a demonstrable speed disadvantage as far as I can tell, but there is a consistency advantage to holding the gun a bit lower than you conventionally would.

Positioning the gun height-wise relative to your body and getting the gun a bit closer to your body than a "full extension" firing position isn't quite enough to ensure a smooth magazine insertion. You also need to take care to angle the magwell properly. Obviously, this is something you should experiment with a bit on your own, but a good place to start is pointing the magwell directly to your magazine pouches. For most people this means a little bit of an unnatural "break" in their wrist as they point the magwell down to the pouches.

Experimentation is important here. Understand what the various options are in terms of gun position and work with them. Please understand that we aren't only training for a good reload in a static position. The goal is to be able to reload while at a run or twisting your body around in potentially awkward positions. Static technique is just the start.

I spent so much time talking about the dominant hand that I didn't give any attention to what the non-dominant hand is doing. Obviously, while your dominant hand dumps the magazine and gets the gun positioned for the next magazine, your non-dominant hand is grabbing a fresh magazine off your belt. When discussing speed, it is your magazine retrieval and insertion speed that is the limiting factor for your reload speed. How quickly you dump the old magazine doesn't usually affect the overall time.

In any case, when retrieving a new magazine from the belt, it is important to grip that magazine in such a way that it is easy to insert into the pistol. Positioning the base-pad of the magazine in the palm of your hand is a sensible solution. If you lay your pointer finger across the front of the magazine (the front is the part that has the noses of the bullets), you should also have the effect of being able to "point" the magazine into the gun.

*Run your hand into the bottom of the trigger guard in order to find your grip again.*

I constantly have guys in classes that grab the magazine with their fingertips, and then try to put the magazine in the gun that way. That is no good.

It just isn't as consistent as getting the basepad into the meat of your hand and working with it that way.

Finally, it is important to re-establish a proper grip on the pistol after reloading. This is an area that many shooters struggle with and don't even really realize it. If you pay attention during your training, you will see that often you will come back up on the gun with a less then optimal, if not just plain bad grip on the gun. The easiest solution for that is to have a step built in to your reloading process where you are going to make sure you get that same consistent grip on the pistol after you stick a magazine in. I like to roll my hand up the gun and run the side of my non-dominant pointer finger into the bottom of the trigger guard. I use that as an index point to let me know that I am back on a good grip and ready to resume shooting. No matter how you grip the gun, it will probably help you to establish an index point on the gun that you know to go to after you reload. It will help build consistency and accuracy.

Even though there is this complicated set of steps, when you get good at reloading it should look like a fluid motion. Just like the draw, look at your reload technique and watch for any extraneous motions. Some shooters like to twist their wrist to flip the mag out of the gun. Some like to bring the gun down onto the magazine as they insert it. Of course, it is pretty well impossible to have literally zero extraneous motion, but you should do absolutely all you can to minimize it. It isn't making you any faster!

If something goes drastically wrong during a reload, there is a good way to minimize the negative impact on your score. By drastically wrong, I am talking about missing the magwell to the point where you lose control of the fresh mag and drop it on the ground. Maybe you just have a really poor grip on the mag and can't get it into the magwell. In a circumstance like that it is usually fastest to simply abandon that magazine and grab another fresh one off your belt. This is a good reason to always have spares.

It is important to discuss some equipment issues related to this. For some divisions in USPSA, shooters are allowed to attach an external magwell to the gun to aid in reloading. Magwells are a serious advantage. They allow the shooter to have a quite a bit more "slop" in the way the magazine is positioned when inserting it into the gun. For a Production shooter like myself, a magwell almost feels like cheating. A magwell is pretty much a must if your division allows it.

The other big equipment issue for reloading is your magazine pouches. I think you can make do with pretty much any popular magazine pouch on the market, but a better pouch does make life easier. I like to be able to get a complete grip on the magazine while it is still in the pouch. This is much the same as being able to get a firing grip on your pistol while it is still in the holster (it aids in a fast and consistent draw). I don't think you should treat your magazines any differently. Do your best to set your pouches up so that each magazine can be gripped completely and independently. If your body is in the way, then try to set the pouch up so it gives you a bit more clearance from your body.

Your magazine pouches should retain the magazines during running (obviously), but be careful that they aren't overtight. You will be slowed down if you need to overcome excessively tensioned magazines in the pouches.

A popular trend in more recent years is using pouches that point the bullets "nose out" away from your body. This configuration is a bit easier to set up so that you can completely and independently grip each magazine, but I think it takes a little bit more work to learn.

In any event, make sure you have your equipment set up so that it works for you instead of against you. If there is some beef you have with your gear, then you should be fixing it instead of working to overcome it through training. You are going to have plenty of other stuff you need to work on.

## From Mike Hughes (USPSA Grand Master, Inventor of SIRT Pistol)

### *The Case for Consistent, Reliable, No-look Reloads*
*Just as you can bring your fingertips together with your eyes closed, your innate ability of awareness of your hands can allow a no-look reload while you maintain your vision on targets and your surroundings. There is no need to look at the gun, so don't bother with it. You don't look at your feet when running full speed do you?*

*With your forefinger extended along your magazine, have an awareness of the second knuckle of your*

Mike Hughes.

*pinkie (or your ring finger if you're shooting a compact pis-*
*tol) and simply bring 'em together to complete a reload.*

*Now try to bring your strong arm elbow down in*
*front of your chest and the gun down so your elbow is*
*consistently pressed against your torso. This aids in sta-*
*bilizing the gun as you accelerate and decelerate at maxi-*
*mum rates (keeping the gun from bobbling around). Note:*
*After you reload, you have to reestablish your grip so that*
*slight extra time to bring the gun back up is done con-*
*currently while reestablishing the grip from your support*
*hand so no time is lost.*

*Practice in all body orientations and for bringing the*
*gun into a reload from as many different arm positions*
*as possible. In time you will nail no-look reloads with*
*subconscious confidence.*

The pro-active type of reloading isn't the only kind you
should master. Often, for a variety of reasons, people end
up needing to reload a completely empty gun. Of course,
this is almost always a mistake. Doing an unplanned static
reload hurts your score about as much as a miss does, but if
you haven't trained a good static reloading technique, then
it could hurt you even more! I have seen plenty of shooters
stress out, and then induce a malfunction when they are
trying to reload an empty gun. Train for this scenario so
you don't turn a minor mistake into a blown match.

The first consideration here is being able to recognize
when your gun is empty. This sounds somewhat silly to
many, but it is important. Not every gun has a working
slide stop, so an empty gun may look just like a loaded
gun. The magazine will be inserted, and the trigger will

just have been pulled, but nothing happened. Your gun may have malfunctioned and still have ammunition in it. There are many equipment issues in play here, and they are outside the scope of this book. The bottom line is that it is important to know your equipment and be able to diagnose what is going on with it. You don't want to waste time trying to apply a solution to the wrong problem. If your gun needs bullets, give it bullets.

Most Production guns come equipped with working slide stops, so we can deal with that scenario now. Up to the point in the reloading process where we come to inserting the fresh magazine, nothing changes. For USPSA purposes, I recommend that most shooters work in an extra step in the reloading process where they deliberately work the slide release after seating the mag. What I mean by this is that the shooter seats the fresh magazine, and then shifts their vision from the magwell to the slide stop. After that, they hit the slide stop with their non-dominant thumb.

This is a desirable technique for a couple reasons. First, the shooter will need to actually seat the magazine (or at least make an attempt at seating it) before they are in a position to work the slide stop. If the shooter uses their dominant hand thumb, it is a fairly frequent mistake (especially under pressure) to thumb the slide release before the magazine makes it into the gun. If you seat the magazine, and then work the slide stop with the same hand, you reduce the possibility of that mistake. Another reason to hit the slide release with the non-dominant thumb is the shooter will have more leverage with that hand in most cases. They will be able to push harder to ensure the slide stop is disengaged.

When considering a technique for reloading an empty gun, it is important to understand that for most USPSA divisions, this is both an unplanned and rare event. Generally speaking, it shouldn't happen in the higher capacity divisions. Shooters using a 1911 in Single Stack Division will likely have this happen much more often. The point here is that if you have driven yourself to have an empty gun, the stress level may well be quite high. You need a dependable technique so you can fix the problem and get back to shooting.

Another important thing to point out with empty gun reloads is that the better shooters will do them while moving. If a mistake is made and some extra rounds were fired in a position, the better shooters are probably already leaving that spot. This means they have a bit more time to be certain they deal with the slide-locked gun properly before they get to the next position. Speed then isn't really as critical as being certain it is done properly.

I said I recommend most USPSA shooters use the "non-dominant thumb slide release" technique, but not all. If you are one of the people that have a gun that will reliably "auto-forward" when a fresh magazine is slammed into the gun, then that technique is plainly fastest. Just remember that technique needs to work for you on your particular gun. If you ever encounter a time in practice or in a match where you auto-forward the gun and it doesn't pick up a round, you may want to discontinue the use of that technique.

Finally, there are many shooters that have guns with very small slide stops that are hard to manipulate under the best circumstances and nearly impossible under stress.

It may well be best to hand cycle the slide to chamber the next round. This is the slowest method, so it is the least desirable option.

For non-USPSA shooters, the priorities are different. For example, IDPA shooters do "slide lock" reloads on a regular basis. They aren't surprise events. Slide lock reloads are a regular fact of life in IDPA. This means those shooters can develop their own techniques that are perhaps a bit quicker for fixing an empty gun problem. There are faster techniques available, but perhaps they aren't quite as reliable.

One possible solution is to "pre-load" the slide release with your dominant thumb. With some pressure on the slide release the magazine being inserted is usually enough to drop the slide forward. This technique works on many guns. The problem with it is that too much pressure on the slide stop will release the slide before the magazine gets into position. Too little pressure and the slide won't drop when the magazine is inserted. This technique is a little risky at a USPSA event. As I explained earlier, running the gun empty usually means you have already made some mistake and that you are probably feeling the effects of match pressure. If you apply too much force to the slide stop and drop the slide before you have the gun loaded, you will make a bad situation worse. In an IDPA context though, the "pre-load" technique may make a great deal of sense. You need to experiment a bit and figure out what works the fastest and most consistently for you.

The best method to practice reloads is to work at home in dry-fire. I strongly recommend dummy rounds in the magazines to get them to the appropriate weight.

The plastic dummy rounds that hardly have any weight to them are a waste of time. Ammunition loaded without powder and primer is much better.

In terms of a performance metric, a good benchmark for most shooters is 1.1 or 1.2 seconds, measured shot to shot at a seven-yard target for a speed reload. One second is really fast for a Production shooter. Limited or Open guns are faster, with the fastest shooters consistently getting under a second.

## From Matt Hopkins (USPSA Grand Master)

### *Working on Reloads*

*There are many different opinions on reload technique, but what all the best practitioners have in common is that they work hard at it. The best in the sport of USPSA put in the work to reload without conscious thought. It takes thousands of repetitions of any skill to make it happen without having to think about it. Personally, I spent years working at it just to be profi-cient. One year I did reload drills for an hour a day! I practiced before I went to work, and then got back to it when I got home in the evening.*

There are a few common mistakes made during reloading. It is common to miss the last shot prior to the reload. This

*Matt Hopkins executes a reload.*

is associated with rushing, and a shooter should work hard at being disciplined in this respect. This mistake shows up commonly on the "stand and blast" type stages such as classifiers. People get in a hurry and mistakes are made.

### Rushing

*During my own training, I have often found myself rushing my shots after a reload. Commonly, your reload is judged by how fast it is, and I want to be fast. When I am pushing for a fast reload time, I often catch myself rushing the shot after the load. I get faster by aiming less. It is good to be more efficient when you are aiming, but that can easily turn into just slinging a shot at the target without aiming at all. Try to watch out for that during your training.*

## From Tim Herron (USPSA Grand Master)

### Reloading the Gun

*I don't get too hung up on individual preferences as long as the technique used is consistent. I shoot left-handed and choose to actuate the magazine release with my trigger finger. It works for me (and very fast mind you) and is the most consistent way for me to activate it when performing my reloads. I primarily*

*shoot in a division that allows a magwell; however, I might add that if you're relying on the magwell to assist all of your reloads, you definitely need to polish your technique. The magwell should only be there to help primarily in the direst of mistakes. The magazines should otherwise insert almost effortlessly with proper technique.*

Another common problem is for a shooter to direct their attention (meaning their eyes) to the next target they plan to shoot in the middle of the reloading process. Most every USPSA shooter will train to look the new magazine into the gun. This is very helpful, especially when moving quickly around a stage. However, when shooters get into that "match pressure" mode, where they are under stress and in a hurry, they start to mess up reloads because they don't look the magazine into the gun.

# SINGLE-HANDED SHOOTING

It is sometimes the case in practical shooting that you are required to shoot one-handed. This could be with your dominant (strong) hand or your non-dominant (weak) hand. Additionally, you may be required to move the gun from one-hand to the other. This is one of those skills that the lower level guys almost never practice, and I think they end up paying the price on match day.

Fundamentally, nothing changes from two-handed shooting. However, single-handed shooting tends to force mistakes and can be the source of quite a lot of complaining. With good technique and diligent practice, you can turn single-hand shooting into a strong point.

Before I get into the actual shooting mechanics, I want to address the issue of how to get yourself set up to shoot one-handed. Sometimes you need to draw the gun from the holster. Sometimes you pick the gun up off a table. Sometimes you need to transfer the gun from one-hand to the other. A little bit of pre-planning and training should help minimize confusion on match day.

The usual thing you will need to do is to draw the gun from the holster. If you are shooting strong hand only, then you shouldn't need to do anything special. Shooting one-handed integrates well with regular draw technique. Simply acquire a firing grip on the gun with your strong hand and bring it up to the target. You don't need to do any additional work. Obviously, this is going to feel a lot different from a regular two-handed draw. Be sure you are training to draw one-handed so you aren't caught in a match doing this for the first time.

If you are required to start holstered, but shoot weak hand only, then you have the additional step of transferring the gun to your weak hand from your strong hand. I like to draw the gun one-handed and bring it up to the same place I would reload the gun. From there, I look at the gun and place the gun in my weak hand. I am careful to be consistent with the positioning of the gun (weak hand all the way up on the beavertail). I personally prefer to draw the gun from the holster with the same grip I always use, and then I get my strong hand thumb out of the way by bringing it off the grip of the pistol. I prefer this method because it is consistent with my regular draw training to the largest extent possible.

Some shooters prefer to change their draw technique entirely when they are going to draw and transfer to the weak hand. They may want to grab the optic on their Open gun, and then place the gun in the weak hand. They may grab the gun down low on the grip frame, leaving the higher part more exposed for the weak hand to grab on to. I think these methods are fine. They might offer an advantage (it is hard to say), but they will require additional training. If you aren't sure what to do, then you may as well do something as similar to your regular draw as possible.

Sometimes you are required to pick the gun up from a table, and then shoot it one-handed. If possible, I like to use two-hands to pick the gun up (in order to ensure a good grip on it), and then carry on shooting one-handed. The stage may not allow you to use your non-firing hand to assist, and that's fine. Be sure you train to use just one-hand to pick the gun up. The key point here is to make sure you get a good firing grip on the gun. Raw speed of your first shot isn't going to be as critical as nailing a solid and consistent grip on the pistol.

With the gun handling concerns addressed, we can move on to the actual shooting mechanics of one-handed shooting. You (hopefully) remember back to the "Grip" section that there was quite a bit of discussion about the effects of having a proper two-handed grip. It is important, first and foremost, to understand all these advantages are stripped away when shooting with only one-hand. The gun will flop around (seemingly) uncontrollably when shooting one-handed. You must be extra careful with trigger control, because you don't have the benefit of a strong grip to help correct for any error in the trigger manipulation. No matter how much you train, you will probably always feel a little bit awkward and slow when shooting one-handed. You should accept that feeling, and work to shoot the best you can.

There are quite a few tricks that people use in order to try to close that performance gap. Some of them work and some of them don't.

First, there are a few grip-related things that you can do when shooting one-handed. The most obvious thing to do is to just grip harder. When shooting with a two-handed grip, most people will not grip the gun as hard as possible with their dominant hand in order to maintain some dexterity with the trigger finger (again, something you should remember from the "Grip" section). When shooting one-handed, you will probably want to switch to gripping as hard as you can. You will not need to pull the trigger as fast as you had to when shooting two-handed. Therefore, you can give up the trigger speed and instead grip the gun much harder in order to fight the recoil. Even the most gamed out 9mm pistol with bunny fart loads will be tough to control with only one-hand on it.

*Pulling your weak hand up to your chest is a good idea.*

When you are gripping down harder on the pistol, it is going to require you to be very careful when it comes to trigger control. Squeezing your hand harder to fight the recoil will often induce your trigger finger to start slamming the trigger harder. You absolutely need to train shooting one-handed while paying very close attention to your trigger finger to make sure you aren't throwing shots one way or the other. Usually, right-handed shooting throws shots left and vice versa. This doesn't tend to happen as much during slow fire shooting, so make sure you are working on this issue while shooting quickly.

Along the same lines of gripping down harder, some instructors assert that moving the thumb down on the grip increases the grip strength. It may be true that in theory, this gives someone a marginally stronger grip, but it is difficult to show that there are any tangible benefits from doing this. I personally don't bother moving my thumb down because it has a home on top of the safety of my pistol. I am always using my thumb to actively disengage the safety. Most 2011 shooters are the same way. If you have a pistol (such as a Glock) that allows you to easily slide your thumb down during one-handed shooting, then you should feel free to experiment with thumb position. You may have a preference one way or the other.

The only finger position that may be sensible to adjust is that of the trigger finger. With the support hand off the gun, it now makes sense to get more leverage on the pistol. Every shooter is built differently, and so is every pistol, but getting more finger into the trigger is going to result in more leverage. The reason that you wouldn't want to do this all that time is that you wouldn't be able to work the trigger as quickly. Again, without support on the pistol, priorities change. Consider moving your finger, especially if you have a heavy trigger on your pistol. Experiment with trigger finger position using the "Wall Drill" that I mentioned in the "Marksmanship Fundamentals" section.

When shooting one-handed, it is a good idea to do something with the hand you aren't using. If you let it hang down at your side, it can create a "pendulum" effect. Truthfully, this isn't a big problem when you are just standing and shooting static. However, if you are carrying a heavy object through a stage, the pendulum effect can be much more serious. It is a good habit to pull the free hand in toward your body. I wouldn't get too comfortable with having your hand in a particular spot. Your hand may be required (by the stage) to pull a rope, or hang on to a wall, or whatever else the Match Director can think up. You need to be ready to adapt to any situation, so you don't want to always train to have your hand in some preferred spot. There is simply no guarantee the stages will allow for that.

It is popular to cant the pistol inward slightly when shooting one-handed. This is another one of those little tricks that people seem to favor that doesn't have much of a tangible positive effect. This does create a point of impact shift with your bullets on long range targets. This isn't a huge issue as you will usually be shooting close range when shooting one-handed, but there is no guarantee the Match Director will take it easy on the shooters. Just because of the point of impact shift, I recommend against tilting the pistol, even if you subjectively find it to be more comfortable.

It does make a certain degree of sense to alter your stance when shooting only one-handed. If you blade your gun side slightly toward the targets, you will improve your range of motion through the targets. By "blading," I mean stepping your gun side closer to the targets. If you recall in the "Stance" section, there is a discussion about keeping the targets you are engaging between the lines drawn out from your feet. With one-handed shooting, this no longer applies. The area where targets can comfortably and effectively be engaged is actually quite a lot larger with only one-hand on the gun.

It is often advised that shooters should lean into the gun quite a lot more when shooting one-handed to get more recoil control. This is almost entirely wishful thinking. If you ever need a demonstration of how your primary means of recoil control is your grip and not your stance, then single-handed shooting is just that demonstration. You can't simply lean into the gun more and have recoil control again. That recoil control comes from your hands being on the gun. This is why people necessarily shoot slower with only one-hand on the gun.

If you are curious about how "good" you can shoot one-handed, then let me give you a couple pointers. You want to maintain acceptable accuracy ("A"s and close "C"s) with only one-hand. Obviously, once the targets get far enough away, it is going to be a tall order to stay on par with your freestyle shooting. I don't think it is too much to ask to maintain good accuracy strong hand only to 20 yards and good weak hand only accuracy to 15 yards. If you can do that, you should be all right in a match.

Shooting at appropriate speed is a little bit trickier. The top-level guys can shoot one-handed as fast as their sights line up on the target. There isn't a delay between the sights coming down out of recoil or the sights coming to a target and the shot breaking. They are able to shoot to what they are actually seeing because they have developed their skills to the point where they can pull the trigger fast and straight with only one-hand on the gun.

The best advice I can offer for learning to shoot single-handed is to train yourself for USPSA style speed shooting. When I watch USPSA shooters prepare for a one-handed shooting stage, they take the speed part out of the equation and simply practice hitting the targets. They shoot slowly, but are very careful about trigger manipulation. This is usually because they have experienced a one-handed shooting stage before, and (while under pressure) they shank shots into the delta zone, or even off the target. They then correctly identify the problem (trigger control), but don't really have a good solution. If you train yourself to pull the trigger straight while you are shooting slowly, then best case scenario in the match you will be slow and accurate. Usually, the time pressure gets to people on match day and they end up rushing and shooting faster than they trained to shoot and end up shanking shots. I strongly believe the best thing you can do is train yourself to shoot quickly with only one-hand.

A good test of this is the classic "Bill Drill" at seven yards, but you shoot one-handed. You draw and shoot six "A" hits on the target in two seconds or less in the classic version of this drill. This is done shooting freestyle. If you want to use this test for single-handed shooting, then you would only add a couple tenths of a second when shooting strong hand only. Your shooting pace is only slightly slower than freestyle. When shooting weak handed, your shooting pace would be the same, you would just have a bunch of time added to the draw to give you time to draw the gun and transfer it to your weak hand. The "Bill Drill" shot one-handed should give you an adequate test and skill builder for one-handed speed shooting.

## Flashlights

"Low light" stages are commonplace in IDPA. Sure, you will have them at USPSA matches occasionally, but it is more commonly seen in IDPA.

*Neck index technique.*

First, there is the "neck index" technique. Neck index is my personal preference on low light stages. All you do is hold the flashlight near your neck with your non-dominant hand. You then do your shooting strong-hand only. This technique is attractive because it doesn't require any specific practice. If you hold the flashlight so that you illuminate the sights and the target, you are all set. The only thing you need to be careful to do is to move your whole upper body as a unit. The light needs to follow the gun, and the gun needs to follow your eyes. Everything needs to move together.

It is important to hold the flashlight so that the bottom of the light it is projecting illuminates the sights, but pointing the light lower than that is counter-productive. The more of the gun itself that you illuminate, the more light you will have reflected back into your face. In a low light situation, that light can nearly blind you if you shine it too low.

The other good option is to trap the flashlight between your non-dominant middle finger and pointer finger. You then try to grip the pistol the same as you normally would. Of course, the flashlight is in the way, so it may not be easy. In my opinion, this technique can produce the best results (because you have a two-hand hold). However, there are problems. Due to differences in the size of the flashlight, the controls, and the size of your hands, this technique may not be viable. It just depends. It also requires practice. Since the light is sometimes provided by the match, you may not get an opportunity to practice. If you train this technique, try it. Otherwise, I would avoid it in favor of the neck index.

*Holding the flashlight between your fingers.*

If the stage is "low light," but not quite "no light," it may be an option to let the light hang by the lanyard (if it has one), and just shoot the stage. The light reflecting off the floor will provide you some reference. This solution isn't perfect because the light swinging around can disorient you.

In any event, when you have a "low light" stage to contend with, you should keep your eyes shut for as long as you can before actually shooting the stage. It takes minutes for your eyes to fully adjust to low light conditions, and you want that process started as soon as possible.

**From Brad Engmann (USPSA Grand Master, author of "Modern Handgun Fundamentals")**

## One-Handed Shooting
*There is a little bit more to shooting one-handed properly than simply removing your support hand from the gun. Managing recoil and delivering accurate follow up shots*

*effectively is based on using leverage and biomechanics to your advantage. Since you are now only holding the gun with one-hand, the direction of those recoil forces are going to impact your body differently. You want to ensure that you get your weight in the correct position and realign your index slightly to account for the fact that the gun will be reacting only against one side of your body instead of both.*

*To achieve a good neutral stance, first, put your shooting side foot forward and place about three quarters of your weight on it. Your support side foot should be staggered comfortably off to the side at about a 7 to 8 o'clock angle, with your hips angled similarly and your feet a little wider than shoulder width. Your torso should be forward of your hips. This will help dramatically in controlling the gun. Now, you should align the bones in your shooting hand naturally to aim the gun. There should be a slight inside "roll" to it, and the gun will not be straight up and down. This is because your arm should sit in the most natural way so as not to introduce auxiliary forces when pulling the trigger. To find this natural angle, simply point at something in the room (as if saying "hey you!"). Notice the hand location? That's what you want. If your support side hand isn't doing anything (like holding a flashlight), then bring it in across your chest for balance. Now bring the gun to your eye and you're ready to shoot.*

# CLEARING MALFUNCTIONS

**D**ealing with pistol malfunctions is a skill set that is often ignored by USPSA shooters. It shouldn't be. No matter how reliable your equipment is, it eventually will malfunction. If you think your gear is perfect, then you should shoot with it more. No matter how much care you give or how good the quality of the gear is, it eventually won't work right. When these malfunctions inevitably occur, the time it takes you to fix them counts as part of your score. For this reason, malfunction clearance is an issue that USPSA shooters should understand and practice in order to minimize the damage to their score when this stuff happens. Now is as good a time as any to point out that the worst possible thing you can do in a malfunction situation is to panic. Figure out the problem and work the problem. Stay calm. That's the best you can do. The more preparation you put in beforehand on how you are going to fix malfunctions, the better prepared and less panicked you will be when it happens to you.

*Many people wonder what they should do after having a malfunction. Go faster? Slow down and get the hits? When you have a malfunction, the damage to your score is already done. All you can do is fix the problem and get back on your plan. You can't make up for lost time, it is gone. Stay cool and move on.*

There are a few different schools of thought on how to best handle malfunctions. The most commonly taught method is as follows:

1.  The gun doesn't go off when the trigger is pulled and the shooter recognizes there is a malfunction.
2.  The shooter initiates the "immediate action" malfunction clearance (sometimes called "Phase 1").
3.  If "immediate action" fixes the problem, fine. If not, the shooter moves to "remedial action" (sometimes called "Phase 2").

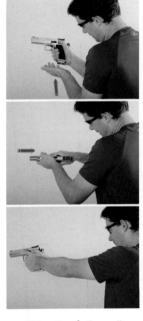

*"Tap Rack Bang."*

In Step 1, the key is that the shooter needs to recognize there is a malfunction. This isn't always as easy as it may sound. Depending on how the gun is set up, it may be difficult to recognize a malfunction. For example, if a gun doesn't have a functioning slide stop, the gun will externally look normal when it runs out of ammunition. I have often seen shooters with Limited guns have a stovepipe and try to reload the gun (thinking they are out of ammo). The sooner you recognize a malfunction, the sooner you can fix it.

Step 2 is the "immediate action" malfunction clearance. This is commonly known as "Tap Rack Bang," or sometimes "Tap Roll Rack," or even "Tap Rack Roll." This procedure is designed to fix most problems that your gun could have had.

The process is simple. The magazine is firmly slapped into the gun with your non-dominant hand. It is possible that if the gun was just reloaded, the magazine was not seated. Sometimes a shooter will inadvertently hit the magazine release, and the magazine will still be in the gun, but not firmly seated. Firmly seating the magazine will fix these potential problems.

After seating the magazine, the slide needs to be cycled. It is usually best to grasp the slide in your non-dominant hand, and then to firmly pull the slide to the rear. The reason to use the whole hand (the "power stroke") technique is that it will provide the most leverage and mechanical advantage. Pinching the slide between two fingers doesn't give you as much grip on the slide. If the gun has some sort of obstruction in the breech, it may be difficult to work the slide to the rear. It is important to get all the mechanical advantage you possibly can. One caution here, avoid covering the ejection port with your hand. If there is a detonation of a round in the gun, you want to try to minimize any injury you might suffer.

If you are performing the "Tap Rack Bang" procedure, then during "racking" the gun, it is also a good idea to hold the gun so that the chamber has a more direct path to the ground. In this way, gravity can aid in clearing out the piece of brass or whatever may be preventing the gun from cycling. It is pretty easy to turn a minor malfunction into a major one by improperly racking the gun. If you "short stroke" the gun, or don't tilt the gun so the spent case or whatever can actually get out of the gun, then you probably aren't helping yourself.

After performing the "immediate action" process, you can then attempt to fire again. If that doesn't work, you need to take "remedial action" (also known as "Phase 2").

"Remedial action" consists of removing the magazine from the gun, cycling the gun until it is clear, putting a new magazine into the gun, cycling the gun, and resuming shooting. This process has some difficulties that can crop up, so it needs to be addressed in more detail.

Removing the magazine from the gun may not be as simple as hitting the magazine release. In fact, when things get to the point of requiring "remedial action," the magazine probably will not fall free from the gun. The magazine will need to be forcibly "stripped" from the gun. The easiest way to accomplish this is to first lock the slide to the rear. The slide will be exerting forward pressure on the magazine and the brass or cartridges in the chamber. That pressure needs to be relieved so that the magazine can be easily removed. Therefore, the first step is to lock the slide to the rear.

*For the magazine stripping step of "remedial action," it has been asserted by some that the most efficient way to remove the magazine may be to hit your dominant side wrist against your non-dominant wrist in such a way that the magazine will be thrown from the gun. If you understand that the magazine may require quite a bit of force to clear from the gun when the slide is still forward, then you will see why this is an inadvisable technique.*

Once the slide is locked to the rear and the magazine is removed from the gun, the gun needs to be cycled until it is clear of all ammunition and spent brass. Typically, people are instructed to cycle the gun three times. This number seems to be more a tradition than based in sound reason. Looking at the gun during cycling makes sense, and once you see the gun is clear you should be able to reload it. Obviously, looking at the gun during a low light situation may not be very helpful, so you just need to rely on racking the gun a few times during that scenario and hope that the problem is solved.

Using a new magazine (if available) instead of the magazine you just stripped from the gun is a good idea. The magazine may have malfunctioned and, in turn, caused the gun to malfunction. It would take time to assess the condition of the magazine, more time than inserting a new one. For that reason, simply putting a fresh magazine (hopefully it will work better) into the gun is the preferred solution.

OK, so there it is. That is the most common training for how to clear malfunctions. The appeal to this paradigm is that it doesn't require much knowledge of the mechanics behind how guns work. This method is taught successfully to people with almost zero experience with pistols and generally they are able to keep their guns working. If you are new to shooting handguns, or even if you are an experienced USPSA shooter, there is some value in learning this technique of addressing malfunctions. Having a plan for when things go wrong is absolutely essential.

The problem with the Phase 1/Phase 2 school of thought is that an awful lot of time may be spent doing things that are not helpful for whatever the problem actually is. For example, a piece of brass may be "stovepiped," preventing the slide from going back into battery. The solution for this problem has nothing to do with slapping the magazine into place. However, the Phase 1 malfunction clearance would be to hit the magazine, and then run the slide, just for simplicity's sake.

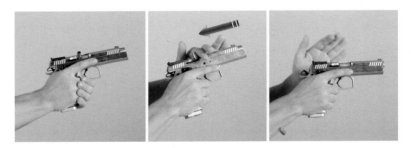

*Clearing a "stovepipe" malfunction.*

The solution to the problem of the time wasted in the Phase 1/Phase 2 techniques is to diagnose the issue that the gun is having, and take only the action needed to fix that problem. Obviously, this requires a more detailed knowledge of how guns work, and it requires you understand what malfunctions are occurring in your pistol and why. I think the tendency is that as shooters gain experience in shooting, they tend to move away from the Phase 1/Phase 2 type of thinking and work toward a diagnose the problem/fix the problem mentality, even if they aren't consciously making an effort to do so.

There is one disclaimer required before we get into this: These techniques are just broad outlines that should work for most pistols. Nobody knows your specific platform better than you do, and I suggest you adapt the techniques you like and throw out the ones you don't. These are just some ideas for you to consider.

The "diagnose, then fix" technique goes like this:

1.  When the gun stops working it is tilted back slightly so the shooter can diagnose the problem.
2.  The shooter looks at two specific places on the gun to diagnose the problem.
3.  The shooter takes corrective action and continues shooting.

Let us work through these steps in order.

First, when the gun stops working for whatever reason, the shooter should break their wrists and very slightly tilt the gun backward. They should tilt the gun back enough so they can see into the chamber of the pistol in order to see what is going on.

Second, the shooter looks at two specific points to figure out what the problem is. The first place is into the chamber, and the second place is the rear of the slide. They are looking to see what is going on in the chamber and if the slide is in battery. This is where things get complicated. The shooter needs to take corrective action based on what they see. Please understand this will take some training. If you spend some time at the range training responses to specific visual stimuli, you will be able to problem solve without having to think about it.

There are a few possible actions that can be taken:

1.  The slide is locked to the rear and the chamber of the gun is empty. The magazine follower is

visible, so the magazine is clearly empty. Clearly, the gun is out of ammunition and you should initiate a slide lock reload. This should remind you of the "Reloading" section where there was discussion about how slide lock reloads need to be distinguished from malfunctions, and this is the reason why.

2.  There is a piece of brass visible sticking up out of the chamber. This is the classic "stovepipe" malfunction. You should "sweep" the brass from the gun using your non-dominant hand. The hand needs to come up over the gun and sweep back over the chamber. It doesn't usually take much force to bring the case out of the gun. Once the case is out, the slide should go back into battery without any further action. Some guns will have this type of malfunction, but the brass will not stick up out the side of the chamber (it will be trapped horizontally). Usually, you can just "pick" the brass from out of the gun using your fingers, and the gun will start working again.

    Some shooters feel they should run the slide to the rear to clear the brass instead of sweeping the brass from the ejection port. This is a good solution, but it does have a drawback. If you pull the slide all the way to the rear, and then let it go back into battery, you will usually lose an unfired cartridge in addition to the empty brass. This isn't a big deal in some circumstances, but if you are in a restricted capacity division, you may well need that round.

3. Everything looks normal. The slide is forward and in battery. A few things could be wrong. There could have been an ammunition malfunction. (If it was a "squib" or you suspect a "squib," stop shooting immediately.) There may have been a primer that didn't function, producing a dud round. This is common with reloaded ammunition. The magazine may not be seated and the gun failed to chamber the next round. The solution to these problems (aside from the squib) is to "tap rack bang." The one caveat to understand here is that if you are using a Limited or Open gun with a disabled slide stop, your gun may simply be out of ammunition and need to be reloaded. You have a training decision to make, if that is the case, since your fixed response to this situation may be to reload the gun and cycle the slide.

4. The slide is slightly out of battery. This is fairly common with some striker fired pistols, especially when they get dirty. The solution is to firmly hit the back of the slide to get the gun to chamber the next round. If this doesn't work, then you may have an oversized or damaged case trying to feed into the chamber, and you need to cycle the slide to clear that out.

5. There are two pieces of brass attempting to occupy the same space in the chamber. This is usually known as a "death jam" and will require "remedial action" as discussed earlier. This is usually caused by a failure for the extractor to pull the brass out of the chamber.

6. The "three point" malfunction, where the round has its nose in the chamber, is clear of the feed lips of the magazine, and is hung up without going all the way into the chamber. Hitting the back of the slide or the bottom of the magazine sometimes works. Racking the slide will induce a "double feed," described in Number 5. If tapping the magazine and back of the slide doesn't work, lock the slide back, drop the magazine, clear the round if necessary (sometimes it will fall out with the magazine), and insert a new magazine.

You may notice with all these things there is a certain amount of equipment specific information. The key to being good at solving problems with your gun is to know your gun. It is extremely common to see shooters struggle with malfunction clearance at matches. I can't count how many shooters I have seen at matches run out of ammunition in a gun that doesn't have a slide stop, reload, and not run the slide again to get a round chambered. These sorts of issues can be fixed through training. I understand that training to fix malfunctions with your gun isn't the high-speed ninja stuff that you want to spend time on, but it can certainly help you place higher in matches.

Most USPSA shooters don't do it, but it is a good idea to set up various types of malfunctions that you can experience and practice dealing with them. You can do drills where you react to the timer, clear a malfunction, and then engage a few targets. It is good preparation to get an idea how long it takes to clear different types of malfunctions and to get some practice doing so. When doing these drills, you should understand there is one thing you can't really practice for and that is being surprised by a malfunction. When you set up a malfunction, and then practice clearing it, you (obviously) know that you are about to clear a malfunction. The element of surprise will commonly add quite a bit of time.

It is common practice when shooters are training that they will quit in the middle of a drill if they have a malfunction. If you want to practice clearing malfunctions, you need to continue with the drill and fight through any problems.

*Result of a catastrophic ammunition malfunction.*

Malfunctions are inevitable. In a high-pressure situation, the added pressure caused by a malfunction can be worse than the time lost to the malfunction itself. I have seen many shooters melt down after a gun problem and turn a problem into a catastrophe. If you train to solve malfunctions, you lessen the chance of this happening to you.

One more thing needs to be said about malfunction clearance. There is no reason not to look at what you are doing. Keeping your eyes on the gun will allow you to figure out what is happening with it. There is no advantage to looking at the target, but looking at the gun might help you. It might give you some piece of information that helps you solve the problem faster.

# SHOT CALLING

Shot calling is not a technique, but it is an important and desirable skill to cultivate. Shot calling has a bit of a murky definition depending on whom you talk to. Usually, people like to define it as "seeing the sight lift" or something like that. I think that is a little bit too restrictive for USPSA, as you don't necessarily need to see the sight lift off a target in order to call the shot. The definition I want to use is this one:

Shot calling is the act of knowing, with as much certainty as possible, where a shot you fired will hit at the moment you fire it.

Note that my definition of shot calling is a bit more expansive than the more common thinking of "seeing the sights lift." That definition is limited by what someone visually sees in the sights. I don't think you should place a limitation like "seeing the sights" in your own definition of shot calling. Shots can be called by other means, at least to a limited degree. Obviously, the sights are the best way to do it, just understand they aren't the only way.

Most people's first exposure to shot calling is that of feeling their hands at the time the shot breaks. When shooters first discover flinching and jerking the trigger and those sorts of things, they almost universally start to feel their own flinch in their hands. When you feel your hands dip down right at the moment the shot broke, you know the shot didn't go where you intended. You might think, *Ah, that was a bad one!* This is rudimentary shot calling at best, but with training, you can do a lot better.

I also want to take the time to disconnect shot calling from accuracy. I think shooters get the two concepts confused. They aren't the same thing. Accuracy is hitting where you want. Shot calling is knowing where you hit. These are different concepts, so don't get them confused with one another. It is true that each one builds on the other. If you become accurate, you should be able to call shots. If you are able to call shots, and possess the slightest desire to hit the target, then you will become accurate.

The reason that shot calling is an important skill to develop is that it is your best means of developing self-diagnostic skills. The portions of this book that dealt with common mistakes that occur during USPSA stages were all diagnosed through shot calling. Things like pulling off a target before you are done shooting it, pressing shots low during speed shooting, and failing to return the sights to the target are all observable for yourself if you are calling your shots. In short, if people make mistakes and are able to see where their shots are going, they can fix their own problems.

In a match circumstance, shot calling is also important for a few reasons. First, and most obvious, with the ability to call shots a competitor can immediately fire extra shots if the circumstance dictates it. It is much faster to sling an extra shot at a piece of steel when you know immediately that you missed it. There is no waiting to hear a "ding" or even worse, waiting for the steel to fall. There is no need to wait for confirmation if you are calling your shots.

Another important reason to develop good shot calling skills is to be certain of what is happening as you are shooting. It is definitely a helpful thing when it comes to moving around on a stage. If you have spent any amount of time at a match, you have probably seen someone running from position to position slowly, while they are looking at targets they already shot at, to make sure there are holes in them. This is a very bad habit. It is a waste of time to be looking at targets you already shot at! However, that habit is eliminated if you already know with certainty where your shots went. Even if you tagged a no-shoot and had to fire a makeup shot, you will know what took place, and you can move on with the rest of the stage.

When we start discussion of movement techniques, one of the most important elements is that you decisively and explosively move from position to position. Being certain of where your shots have landed is a great way to move decisively.

Shot calling is important, yes, but how exactly do you learn to call shots?

Before you start really working on calling your shots, I think you should get two key things in place.

1.  Learn to shoot accurately with no time limit.
2.  Stop blinking.

If you are able to hit reasonable targets at whatever distance, say an "A" zone at 25 yards (with no time limit), then that should be accurate enough that you can start working on calling your shots. If you can't do that, you will probably get frustrated at even trying to figure out where

shots are going as you are shooting. There is, unquestion-
ably, some other technique things going wrong, and you
need to get that stuff sorted out before you can effectively
learn to call shots.

The other important thing to get sorted out is your
blinking. If you are going to visually call shots based on
the sight position, then you need to quit blinking every
time you fire. You can have someone check you for blinking by having them look at your eyes (from the side) while
you are shooting. If you are called for blinking, then pay
attention to your face muscles as you shoot. You should be
able to feel your muscles tense up when you blink. If you
focus on your muscles and keep them still while you shoot,
it should put a stop to the blinking.

If you are still having trouble with blinking, then
another exercise many people find helpful is to shoot with
no target in the equation at all. What I mean by this is you
should point your gun into the backstop and watch the
sights while you fire. You shouldn't aim at a specific point
on the backstop (not a rock, not a bunny, nothing). Just
point the gun somewhere safe and make it your goal to see
the sights for the entirety of their recoil cycle.

Once you are shooting accurately and seeing the sight
position, you should be calling shots. If you see the sights
on a target, break the shot, and the bullet doesn't end up
there, then you didn't really see your sights at the moment
the shot broke. You were fooling yourself. This happens to
most people frequently.

Frequently, I get questions like "What is a good shot
calling drill?" or "How can I learn to call my shots better?" These are tough questions to answer because shot

calling is something that you will continually develop in the context of working on general shooting skills. There are a couple little exercises you can do specific to shot calling (like shooting with no target and observing the sight movement), but for the most part you work on shot calling like you work on trigger control, stance, and the rest of it. It all needs to be working for you all the time, and you tend to improve little bits at a time in each area. You just need to keep looking for your sights as you are shooting, and then make a mental note of where you think that shot went. When you check the target, you will know for sure if you were right. Keep looking for your sights. They are there, right in front of you. You just need to pay attention to see what is going on.

Another bit of advice I can give in terms of development is that if you have a drill that mixes in long targets with close target in the same drill. Starting with a drill like this, with long targets, develops good sight awareness and shot calling skills. I think this is because they necessarily must get on the sights for the long targets, and then when they go to the close ones, they can switch to high-speed target focused shooting. They usually retain good awareness of the sight position and sight movement. If you want to develop shot calling, I strongly recommend working far to near on different arrangements of targets while paying close attention to sight alignment.

Provided you can shoot with a high degree of accuracy, you can try another exercise. Set up a target at whatever distance you find convenient, intentionally misalign your sights to various degrees, and then fire a shot. You can try putting the front sight way up out of the notch, jammed over to one side of the notch, or whatever else you care to think of. You should do this at various distances. Most people are surprised at the degree of misalignment their sights can have and still produce acceptable hits. This exercise can help you connect dots in your brain between what you are seeing and where the bullets are hitting.

*Don't misunderstand: Many people think that calling their shots means that the shots are going where they intend. It doesn't mean that. Calling shots is about knowing where the shots went. Just because you are calling the shots, that doesn't mean they will go where you want. It does place you on the path to improvement, though.*

Once you have a good idea of where your shots will hit with live ammunition, you should be able to develop your ability to see your sights all the time in dry-fire. Diligent dry-fire will help you be able to develop the ability to see your sights on targets in a flash and know where those rounds would have gone if you had actually fired them.

The eventual goal is to be able to see the sights almost continuously. Top-level shooters can run the gun as fast as they can pull the trigger and see the sights the entire time. The sights may not be right where they want them, but they see them and know (more or less) where the bullets are going.

Most top shooters are able to have a very good idea where their bullets went during a stage. Some shooters don't even need to follow the score keeper around because they already know where the holes are! As a matter of fact, if you see a shooter on the Super Squad unload after shooting a stage, and then walk directly out to one specific target, it is a safe bet they are afraid they picked up a penalty on that target because they weren't able to call their shots on it.

*The best shot calling I have ever done in my life was in a major match situation. The stage had four targets with everything "hardcovered" except for the "A" zone. These targets were set far enough back that many people suffered misses. I decided I wasn't going to shoot fast or shoot slow; I was just going to call my shots like my life depended on it. If I called a shot out of the "A," I would fire another at that target.*

*As I was shooting the stage, I was confident I knew where every round was going. My eyes had a really sharp focus on the front sight blade. It was almost as if my vision switched to super high definition for a few seconds. Even though I couldn't see the holes in the target, I knew where my bullets were going.*

*I fired two extra shots over the course of the stage. The extras happened subconsciously as a response to seeing my sight move into the black. When I reviewed the targets, I could see I needed both of those extras. In years of training, it has only come together for me that perfectly a handful of times.*

I will leave the "Shot Calling" section with this. You must actively try to see your sights in recoil in order to see them. So many dudes come to a class with me, and it is clear to me that they have convinced themselves that they can't shoot that accurately, or can't shoot that fast or whatever.

I am telling you now that if you look for your sights you will see them. If you see them, you will learn. This will initially involve effort on your part, but it is worth it. I understand that the idea of shooting .20 splits and seeing the sights the whole time sounds like voodoo magic to some people, but I can assure you it is real life, and you can do it too.

# POSITION SHOOTING

From time to time in USPSA, you will need to shoot from an awkward position. Usually, you need to get into this position on the clock and sometimes get back out of position on the clock. You may need to lean around a wall, shoot from a little port, or do any number of uncomfortable things. This is one of the things that make USPSA so dynamic. You never really know what challenges you will encounter. There are some ways of dealing with these challenges generally, as well as some specific techniques for the more specific challenges.

It is important to understand right up front that for most USPSA stages you can't be forced to shoot any particular way. USPSA is "freestyle" after all, and that is an important point. The only thing a USPSA Match Director can do is to construct the stage in such a way  that you don't have much choice but to shoot from a really awkward position.

Generally speaking, the most important thing to remember when shooting from any uncomfortable shooting position is that all of this stuff comes down to marksmanship skills. There isn't some trick that is going to save you from having to know how to shoot. When in an awkward position, your normal stance is disrupted. Even more importantly, the upper body position that you train to use normally is changed. These things change the way the gun recoils, and that change can be dramatic. Instead of your gun recoiling in a predictable fashion, it may seem to be acting crazy. The key to success when shooting from these positions is to just shoot as fast as the sights are telling you that you can. This may feel slow. Don't worry about that, it feels slow for everyone else too.

Aside from having the discipline to "shoot your sights" when confronted with a difficult position, another element that is important is to maintain as much of your normal stance as possible. If you need to lean, for example, just lean as much as you have to in order to reach the targets. Don't lean more than that, it won't help.

### Discipline

*For me, awkward positions have always been a question of disciplined shooting. It may be uncomfortable or unnatural or whatever, but you need to wait for the sights to line up in order to hit the target. It is so common for people to feel "too slow" when the position is awkward. When that happens, they sometimes start rushing, and that is when mistakes happen. You don't want to be that person.*

*Bending the knees helps lean around the wall.*

Aside from keeping your stance as consistent as you can, you need to remember the stance guidelines. We want mobility, stability, and comfort when dealing with tough positions, just as much as we want these things when standing and shooting normally. If you are working into a position, think about the best way out of that position (provided that it isn't the end of the stage). Think about adjusting your foot position, or whatever, to be a bit more stable or comfortable. Think about maintaining that forward weight bias. All of the same considerations that apply to standing and shooting normally also apply to working from an awkward position.

Another general bit of advice I can give is to try to get into a position where you can see all the targets you plan to shoot from one view. For example, if you need to lean around a wall and shoot a few targets, your natural inclination is probably to stop leaning when you see the first target, then shoot that target, then lean a bit more until you find the next one and so forth. This is a time waster. If you can see all the targets you plan to shoot at once, the transitions will be much more efficient. Get into the habit of setting yourself up where you can see everything from one view if you possibly can.

*The stance guidelines always apply.*

The last general bit of advice is to maintain a firm grip. I am not entirely sure why, but most people naturally loosen up their grip on the gun when they get in to an awkward position. You might need to consciously tell yourself to keep your normal firm grip on the gun, but the payoff will be worth it. The sights will track better, and you should be able to shoot faster and more accurately.

## Walls

Leaning around walls is one of the common (if not the most common) things you will see at a match. Depending on the angle of the lean required to get around the wall, it can be extremely difficult to reach the targets. It may also be really easy to get to the targets. It just depends on the specific scenario.

The most important element of leaning around walls is that you get your feet in the right position to begin with. This isn't much of a challenge when inspecting the stage, but when moving full speed into a position under match pressure, it is something that frequently goes wrong. The key thing you can do to ensure that your feet end up in the right spot is to work a step into your stage programming where you place your feet exactly where you want them. This may sound simple, and it is, but many people sim-ply don't do this, and they end up in a position they can't shoot well from. If you have someone recording you while you shoot stages in a match, you should care-fully review the footage. Were you in the best spot to shoot the targets or not? Depending on the difficulty of the position, having your foot three inches one direc-tion or the other can make a huge difference in how easy it is to shoot.

Another important consideration when leaning around walls is to minimize the changes to your upper body. Any change to your upper body will change the feel of the recoil and slow your shooting down while you spend extra time tracking your sights. Obviously, sometimes you need to dramatically twist yourself up in order to reach targets around tough leans, but you should work to minimize any stance disruption. Use your knees as much as you can to help you reach targets, then your waist, and your last resort is to break your "upper body triangle" by compromising your arm or wrist position.

## From Tim Herron (USPSA Grand Master)

*Positioning yourself at a wall edge or barricade, try to ensure that you open your feet to that edge. That is to say, try to align the center of your body to the edge of the wall/barricade. This allows you to better position*

*yourself to shoot around the obstacle and not be so "off-balance."*

*If you are to stand behind a barricade and are going to shoot around the right side, while facing the barricade, pull your right foot back to angle the center of your body to the right edge of the wall. This allows you to shoot farther around the barricade.*

## Low Ports

Frequently, shooters will be required to shoot from a "low port." A low port is just a hole in a wall that is close enough to the ground that the shooter needs to squat or kneel to effectively shoot through it.

It bears repeating that fundamentally your shooting doesn't change. You are just going to be shooting through a port from a more awkward position. Watch your sights and expect it to take a little bit more time for them to track. You may also notice they don't track the same way as standing freestyle shooting. Don't worry about it, just be disciplined and handle it the best you can.

The most important specific consideration when dealing with low ports is whether to select a kneeling position or a crouching position. I can briefly describe the advantages and disadvantages of each choice:

Crouching is going to by far be the more common choice. Crouching is fast to get into and to get out of. Crouching also gives you a wider field of motion. It will generally make for faster transitions from one target to the next due to the increased field of motion you have.

On the other hand, kneeling is generally slower to move into and out of. It can be more comfortable and stable, depending on the specifics of how the stage is set up. Usually, the lower you need to get down, the more likely it is you will want to put a knee down for stability.

If you aren't sure whether you should kneel or crouch, then you should spend some time on the practice range experimenting with different scenarios. You can adjust the height of ports, try different target types, and so on. In a few hours you can get comfortable with all the options you have. I don't want to get too specific about advice in these areas because it varies so much from shooter to shooter. There are plenty of older shooters, shooters with injuries, young and flexible shooters, and plenty of variation in sizes and builds. There isn't a one size fits all solution except to say that if you feel comfortable crouching, then do it so you can avoid taking a knee.

Be sure you carefully plan your exit strategy from a low position. If you are set with your feet really wide while you are shooting, then you may have an easier time getting out of position if you narrow up on the exit. It will be easier to push yourself up from a narrow base, rather than a wide base. Just decide if you need to put your feet closer together on the exit or not based on the position.

One more thing that bears mentioning is when kneeling, you need to consider the terrain. Matches will often have gravel or other extremely uncomfortable range surfaces for the shooters to contend with. Jamming your knee down onto a jagged rock is not fun. Best practice is to keep a kneepad in your range bag at all times for just such an occasion. If you don't have the right equipment to kneel down, you may have to crouch when kneeling would have been better. Don't make that mistake.

## Narrow Ports

Occasionally, you will encounter a narrow slit in a wall. These narrow openings may be just a few inches wide. While these types of ports aren't terribly common, it is important to understand the challenge they pose.

The biggest problem with narrow ports is they make it difficult to locate the targets. Of course, during the stage inspection period you will have a chance to find the specific location of the targets. However, that is a much different thing than being able to find them immediately when you come charging into a position. It is easy to waste tenths of a second here and there while you hunt for targets. You should devote extra visualization time to these sort of ports

*Shooting through a narrow port. Notice only one eye can see the target.*

so you waste as little time as possible when you are actually shooting the stage.

Another challenge that narrow ports pose is that they often are so narrow that you can't see the target with both eyes. This can cause problems with someone's vision. They may be sorting out seeing a "ghost" image of the wall in the way of the target, or maybe the target will appear as a "ghost" behind the solid wall. In any event, this can slow people down as they sort out the confused images their eyes are sending their brain. I usually switch to shooting with just one eye open to sidestep this problem.

Another potential issue is touching the slide of your gun on the port. This is easy to do when the port is narrow. The problem is that the port will interfere with the normal operation of the gun and possibly induce a malfunction. Again, take great care during your walkthrough time to make sure you keep your hands/gun out of contact with the walls so you don't run into this problem on the clock.

## Prone

Prone shooting is unusual at most USPSA matches. Many shooters hate to practice it, and Match Directors tend to take a lot of static if they include prone shooting in a match. However, there are many options for how to go prone and how to shoot once you are on the ground. This isn't stuff you want to figure out on match day, so please do some homework on prone shooting!

In a speed event like USPSA, there isn't time to mess around. The fastest technique to get down prone is to simply throw yourself on the ground, but use your non-dominant hand to break your fall and let yourself down onto the ground. How aggressively you throw yourself on the ground depends on your comfort level with the technique for doing it and the specifics of the range surface. You may be dealing with grass, gravel, or whatever else. Even if the range surface looks soft during the walkthrough you may pepper it with brass while you are shooting the stage. Be careful! It isn't worth getting injured just to get down a couple tenths quicker.

Once you are on the ground, you have a few choices. When the targets are far away, it is best to get your arms and the gun all the way down onto the ground.

Generally, the lower down you are the better. You can rest your cheek on your arm to really get behind the sights. This technique will offer the most stability and accuracy. On the other hand, you will need to reposition your entire body if you need to make anything but the smallest transition from target to target.

For mid-range targets, it isn't necessary to have all the stability of having your arms firmly planted on the ground.

In that situation, you can keep your arms off the ground completely. You will be able to move your arms freely and transition quickly from target to target.

For close range targets, you may want to consider propping your body up off the ground slightly with your non-dominant hand. You will be forced to shoot strong hand only, but you will be able to transition across a fairly wide area very quickly. You will rarely be able to employ this technique, but when it is appropriate, it is a real time saver.

## Prop Manipulation

Occasionally, it is a stage requirement to manipulate a particular prop or to move a prop from one place to another. The possibilities with this are only limited by the imagination of the Match Director. Some would say these possibilities are only limited by how mean the Match Director is. In any event, there are some things that really need to be thought about.

First, we can discuss the possibility of just needing to manipulate a prop. This includes things like opening doors, flipping levers, pushing buttons, pulling ropes, and so forth. As I explained earlier, the possibilities are virtually endless.

Generally speaking, taking care of that prop is going to be done without you shooting anything. You simply grab something and pull or push or whatever you need to do. People have a tendency to want to multi-task. Often, I see people want to push a button while shooting a target. Trying to shoot while manipulating a prop is generally a really bad idea. The usual outcome is to shoot slowly and to ineffectively manipulate that prop. In the chapter on "Training Your Focus" later on in this book, you will find a detailed explanation of these issues. It will be enough for now to say that you want to make sure the prop is dealt with, and then smoothly shift your focus to the next task you have.

Think about it like this. You practice all these different shooting techniques during your training time. You can train all you want, combine different mechanics in unusual ways, and try to be prepared for anything the Match Director throws at you. No matter how much you work at this, you can't be perfectly prepared for every possibility. The easiest way to deal with this is to get to something familiar. Get to what you know how to do. Don't be the guy trying to mess around with some prop in some weird way because it might save you half a second. If there is any doubt at all, get the weird stuff out of the way so you can get back to shooting.

Occasionally, you will be required to hold a prop in your hand in order to force you to shoot strong hand only or weak hand only. In those circumstances, the best advice anyone can give is to assume your normal one-handed shooting position. If you can pull the prop in close to your body as was recommended in the "Single-handed Shooting" section, then do it. If not, make the best of it.

**Other Positions**

The varieties of positions or challenges that a practical shooter will face are virtually unlimited. There isn't an effective way to deal with them all in the context of a book, but there is some important advice that can be given.

Keep things simple. When you encounter something unexpected or new, just come up with the simplest solution you can and focus on shooting the targets you need to shoot. No matter what happens, practical shooting is about shooting. Never let the things you encounter on a stage break your focus on what is really important. Props and shooting positions are just smoke and mirrors designed to distract you from shooting. Don't fall into that trap.

# START POSITIONS

One thing that you tend to see at matches is a substantial variety of start positions. USPSA would be a lot simpler if every stage started with a draw on a target directly in front of you. It would also be quite a bit more boring.

Generally speaking, the Match Directors just want to mess around with your hand position. Maybe your wrists start above your shoulders. Maybe your hands start on a wall. Start positions like that are quite normal. Sometimes they drag out a chair for you to sit on and start from. In a club match setting, it may be no more complicated than any of that.

It is especially common in larger matches to have more of a variety of start positions used. Your gun and/or magazines may start staged somewhere. There could be cars to start in. You may even start lying down. The only limit to any of this is the Match Director's imagination.

I have a few little tips and techniques for some of the more common start positions. When the stage is strange, the important thing to do is to come up with a plan that gets you to familiar techniques. For example, you may encounter a stage where you need to push a button that opens a door before you draw the gun. You should be well versed in how to draw the gun, so that will be easy.

All you need to do is push the button, and then get to what you know. Different start positions are usually just smoke and mirrors like this. Do what you need to do to get to what you know. After that, it should be easy to do what you know.

**Different Hand Positions**
As I said, the most common variation you will encounter is that of a change in your hand position. Wrists above shoulders, hands at sides, hands on a wall, and many more are all just hand position variations. If you reference "The Draw" section, you will see that the technique is designed for this sort of variation. Just get to "Step 1," and you will be all set. After that, nothing changes.

*A few common start positions.*

This may seem self-evident, but it bears repeating. Your practice needs to reflect what you actually need to do in a USPSA match. Don't be the guy that only trains hands at sides. You should regularly work with different hand positions just so you have a feeling of comfort and familiarity no matter how the Match Director makes you start.

At a recent match, I felt a bit uncomfortable with a "wrists above shoulders" start, so my next practice session was entirely wrists above shoulders, just so I would feel normal working from that position.

One little trick that can help with different hand positions is to do a couple of dry grasps of your pistol right after you holster it during your "make ready" routine. It helps get you familiar with your exact gun position during those final moments right before you shoot a stage.

*Something to consider: Many shooters find it helpful to have a reference point for the more common start positions memorized. For example, if the position is "wrists above shoulders," you always put your fingers on your hearing protection. Little tricks like this can help you feel much more comfortable with different start positions.*

**Table Starts**

The gun and/or magazines may start on a table. This is something that you can practice, but Match Directors always seem to come up with a twist that you can't anticipate. Even if you can practice the start position, you may not do it the way it is at the match. Every table is a different height; the range surface can be different, and so on. Even if you can't practice this to the exact detail the way you will encounter it in a match, try it. You can at least be

sure that you don't have too large of a magazine release on the gun or some other catastrophic problem waiting to happen.

When you get to the match, the easiest thing to do is look straight at the gun until you pick it up. Once the gun is in your hands, it will be familiar territory. I make a point of using both hands to pick the gun up (if possible). I want to get a nice solid grip on the gun so I can actually hit stuff when I start shooting.

When you place your gun and mags on the table, you are usually allowed some flexibility as to how you do that. I always place the gun and mags so that I will be able to pick them up just as they would come off my belt. Since I am right handed, I put the gun on the table left side down. My magazines are placed on the table bullet nose up. It is important to have your gear set up to come off the table easily.

Be sure you lay out extra ammo. I have had an extra magazine on a table save my bacon at a match more than once. You never know what might happen; you might drop one on the ground or pick up a magazine that just plain isn't working in your gun. In any event, get extra ammo onto the table!

### Chair Starts

If you start seated in a chair, figure out if you are going to stand up and start shooting right away or maybe move to a shooting position and shoot from there. You can then set yourself up to either move out of the chair quickly, or be able to easily access your gun, whichever appears to be more important.

Beware of the magazines in your rear pouches. You don't want them getting caught in the chair behind you. Some Match Directors are tough and make you start with your back against the back of a folding chair. This puts you in a position where if you stand up straight, your rear magazine pouch could snag on the chair. Be extremely careful in these situations, because you don't want to train wreck the stage or DQ because the back pouch tries to bring a chair along with you for the stage. This might make for a funny YouTube video, after the fact, but it isn't a good thing.

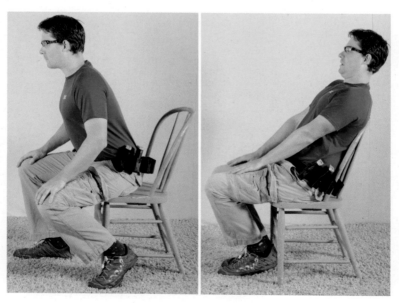

*A couple common chair starts.*

## Bed Starts

When you start lying on a bed, you almost certainly will not have your gun holstered. This means you need to move out of the bed as aggressively as you can to get to the gun. I have found that I usually need to get one foot on the ground, and then use that foot to power off the bed. At the minimum, get off your back immediately. Get your legs swinging off the bed and get moving.

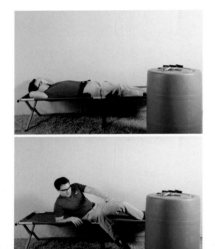

Bed starts are a good time to relentlessly game the start position. Listen to the instructions carefully. Do you need to have your back on the bed? Both your feet? Comply with the start position as minimally as possible so you can get off the bed and get to the noisy part of the stage.

## The Bottom Line

It is probably extremely helpful for your state of mind to view an oddball start position as nothing but a distraction. It is something that happens before you start shooting. If the start position is awkward or even stupid, don't worry about it. Everyone will feel awkward and slow while they get to their gun. Just get at the gun and get started shooting the stage.

# POSITION "ENTRY" AND "EXIT"

If you chose to conceptualize a stage as shooting from one spot and then running and shooting from another spot, then this section will explain how you can properly get in and out of each spot. The techniques explained in this section are the primary reason why top shooters don't need to be world-class athletes to be competitive. Instead of needing to run like a sprinter from one spot or another, they can almost glide in and out of positions while engaging targets the whole time. Properly done, it doesn't look all that fast, but it is efficient.

There are a few issues that need to be addressed before I get too deep into this.

First, there are many schools of thought on how to enter and exit positions on a stage. Some instructors will teach certain things about which foot to lead with into a position and other instructors will admonish students who use that technique. There are a few different schools of thought on this and more than one valid way to do this. The key for you is to pick a system that you understand and that you can learn. I tend to favor having a simple system over having something a bit more complicated.

Second, these techniques are predicated on your other shooting techniques. To be able to move quickly from one spot to another efficiently, you need to be able to reload fast, you need to be able to shoot while moving, you need to be able to call shots, etc. If you can't do that stuff in isolation, you are going to have a hard time doing it in a really dynamic situation. Just keep in mind that all those shooting techniques are what make you effective with movement techniques, not the other way around.

With those issues out of the way, we can get into position entry/exit technique.

Fundamentally, these techniques are about three things:

1. Be ready to shoot as soon as possible when you arrive at a shooting position.
2. "Set up" to shoot from your regular freestyle stance.
3. Get moving from a shooting position as soon as possible.

## From Dave Sevigny (Multiple USPSA and IDPA National Champion as well as IPSC World Champion)

*Dave Sevigny.*

*Practical shooting is about Accuracy, Power, and Speed-DVC. From the moment the starting buzzer sounds to the final shot taken, you need to hustle! The stop and go nature of USPSA or any practical shooting sport means you have to make efficient entries BEING READY TO SHOOT, use proper balance to engage an array, and load for an explosive exit. Staying low, with the gun up when you come in for a landing after an aggressive move, will set you up for a clean presentation.*

I want to describe for you an idealized process. There are many other issues and many caveats, but this process is basically the way things should look and feel.

When you shoot from any position, you get into your regular freestyle stance. This means you stand square to the targets with a little bend in your knees. You should stand in a "fighting" stance, ready to move. If you stand fully erect with no bend in your knees, notice you will need to crouch down in order to explode from that position. This is something you can avoid by crouching down a little bit to begin with. You want to be ready to move without delay.

When you are done shooting from that position, you explode in the direction you want to go. There should be no delay when you decide to move. No time spent loading your weight on one foot or another. You should be standing in a position you can comfortably move from. When you move, you move quickly, as fast as your legs can push you.

A few steps from your next shooting position, you start to decelerate and get the gun up in your firing position. You use the sights, letting them determine when you start shooting. Your knees act like stabilizers, keeping your sight picture from bouncing around. You set up and again shoot from a solid freestyle position, ready to move again.

The basic process probably doesn't seem all that complicated. You set up, you shoot, you move, you get ready, and you shoot again. There isn't much to it at the base level. The problem is there are a few variables that mess with the formula. You move different distances between targets. The targets that you move in and out on are going to be of different difficulties. This may open up the possibility of moving while you shoot the targets. You may need to reload between shooting positions. You may not be moving in or out of a proper "freestyle" platform stance; it may be an awkward position or a lean. Any one of these variables can change the basic formula. Not to mention, people make all sorts of mistakes when it comes to movement, and those mistakes need to be addressed.

## The Sights Tell You What to Do

When it comes to getting in and out of position quickly and efficiently, the sights tell you what to do. If you come into a position and you are staring at a target, but the sights aren't on the target, then you were late bringing the sights up. It is as simple as that. If you leave a position, but didn't see a sight picture for your last shot, then you probably just shot a miss. No matter what, the sights are going to tell you the story of what is going on. If they are bouncing around too much when you are trying to shoot a target, then use your knees better to stabilize things. If you have a good sight picture, but you aren't shooting, then you are wasting time.

## Having the Gun up Isn't Always Enough

It is often the case that I will see shooters run into a position with the gun held up high, but not using the sights. (I have been shooting long enough that I can usually tell the difference.) Having the gun up isn't enough! If the gun is up high, put the sights on target and start aiming. Don't waste the opportunity.

If you have a long distance to run and/or really tough shooting to do when you get to the next position, you should consider holding the gun high up when you get to the next position, but not holding it at full extension aimed at the target. The reason for this is that it is tough to have the gun at full extension and stable when you need to stop yourself after a long run. You might be better off getting your body stabilized before you get the gun out. The reason for this is if your gun is fully extended, it is more prone to bouncing. A little bit of experimentation can help you figure out when to get the gun high and start aiming versus when to get the gun high and wait to stabilize a bit before you push the gun out to full extension.

## Look Where You Are Going
If you have a bit of a move, say five yards or so, then it is helpful to look where you are going. You can program this into your stage plan as well. Just think of the movement as the next thing you need to do after you shoot a target and look where you need to go. Putting your eyes where you are headed helps focus your mind on exploding toward that position. It removes thoughts about what happened in the last position. Just move!

## Point Your Hips Where You Are Going
A good rule of thumb for movement is to point your hips where you are going. This gets your body turned so you can use your big thigh muscles to help quickly push you

in the direction you want to go. You should avoid running sideways because it is awkward and slow.

## Shot Calling Helps

You will be able to move much more surely and aggressively if you know where the shots you are firing land on the targets. This is a big reason why good movement skills are predicated on good shooting skills. The surer you are of what you are doing, the less hesitation there will be when it is time for you to move.

## Keep Your Torso Rigid

You want to use your ab muscles to "zip up" your torso and keep your upper body rigid. What this will do for you is keep your torso from dragging behind your body and making it more difficult for you to move.

## Drop Stepping

Sometimes you aren't able to stand in a comfortable free-style position where your feet are already in a position to help push you. You can't always have a good bend in your knees, because you might finish a shooting position leaning one way or the other. In this circumstance, you should consider doing a "drop step," where you step one foot out to help push you the direction you want to go. It is legal to step over fault lines, so long as you don't fire a shot, so don't neglect this possibility.

## Both Hands on the Gun

You need to be ready a couple steps before you get to a shooting position. You want both hands on the gun and the sights up on the target or where you know the target will appear. In my opinion, it is a bit better to be ready a little early rather than ready a little late. For this reason, on short moves you may want to keep both hands on the gun. This helps keep you ready before you get to the next position. Of course, if the movement is small enough, then you may not even pull the gun down out of your firing position and instead elect to put it straight up on the next target. Experimentation is key to help you figure this stuff out.

## How to Handle Reloads

When you move, you will often have to reload at the same time. Unless the distance you need to move is very short, then you should prioritize moving as fast as you can, and then sort out the reload. Do not artificially slow down your running so you can have an easier time reloading. Get your reloading up to snuff, so you can run full tilt and still get the gun loaded before you get to the next position. This may feel messy or uncomfortable, but it is demonstrably faster than slowly moving and comfortably reloading.

## No Flamingo

Keep your feet close to the ground to minimize extraneous movement. It is not efficient to raise your foot more than a couple of inches off the ground. It takes extra time to raise the foot, and it takes extra time to return the foot to the ground. It forces your torso to compensate by leaning away to provide balance, which diminishes alignment and diminishes explosive power. It decreases the amount of power loaded into muscles the longer the foot is held off the ground. Many shooters get caught in this "flamingo" stance while preparing to move from the last target in the array. It is slow and it doesn't look cool.

### Elevation Changes

You should avoid unnecessarily changing the elevation of your head or shoulders while you move through a stage. This is especially true when you get in and out of positons.

When you leave a position, try to avoid crouching down as you push out. This takes time and is indicative of not being in the proper athletic shooting position in which you can quickly move where you want to move.

When you come into position, you should also watch for the elevation changes. If you "stand tall" as you set up in a position you are changing the relationship of the target to your eye, to your sight. There is no reason to do that. Not to mention, when you "stand tall" in a shooting position, you'll just need to get low again before you move.

### Keep the Upper Body Triangle

Take care that you don't break your upper body position early. I see this happen often when I am pushing students to get out of position faster. As soon as you start pulling your arms in (in a hurry to leave a position), then all bets are off on the shooting part. People tend to miss the targets high when they do this.

### Shoot in and Out If You Can and It Offers an Advantage

It is possible to "shoot in" and "shoot out" of positions where you are shooting on-the-move, a little bit on the way in and out of the position. This is something you see top shooters do regularly. As your skills develop, this will offer more of an advantage to you. You should experiment with this in practice to see if it is viable for you.

Target difficulty is a big variable here. You need to be comfortable with the difficulty of the target, so you can get in and out of position while you are shooting aggressively. Tiptoeing in and out of position while you are shooting isn't going to save time. You need to move fast enough to make it worth it.

*Where to put your feet: Many people seem resistant to the idea that there really isn't a specific choreographed foot position technique that is going to give them some sort of advantage. Unfortunately, there doesn't seem to be, and if there is an advantage, it is so small that the shooting related stuff washes it out. For example, in years of study, I have been unable to determine if there is a difference between "cross stepping" out of a position and "pushing off with your trail foot." I have determined these sorts of questions (while perhaps interesting) don't lead to better shooting or better movement. They lead to dogma.*

When working with students, I find it very common that they are looking for the benefit of proper position entry/ exit technique to be a lot more self-evident than it really is. What I mean by that is, a student can do something that we would both agree is wrong and have it occasionally produce a good result. When you start dealing with more complicated techniques, and then necessarily more complicated drills to teach those techniques, it becomes really difficult to have the timer or the holes in the target tell you a consistent story about the effect your technique is having. When there are many variables in play, sometimes some strange things happen. What is important is that you are patient when learning these techniques, and eventually you will realize the performance gains you are looking for.

*If you find the preceding bit about the "story the timer and the targets tell" being deceptive is confusing, consider this example: When shooting the movement drill that I described in detail earlier, someone may run full tilt into the shooting area, and then throw the gun up in front of their face and start blasting. By luck or divine intervention, they manage to hit all "A"s on the drill and have a fast time. They might then believe that the best technique is just what they did. They think they should always run in full tilt and not worry about finding their sights. They are kidding themselves.*

# MOVEMENT

So, we have on the table the fundamentals of good position entry and exit technique. Start shooting sooner and leave while still shooting. There are some other important questions that need to be addressed . . . questions like "How do I run?"

I am going to define movement narrowly for the purposes of this book. "Movement" is when you are running from one spot to another with nothing else to do. You aren't engaging targets, you aren't reloading, you aren't doing a position "exit" or "entry," you are just running. If you give that some careful consideration, you will probably realize that this isn't the sort of thing that you do on every stage. After all, you are almost always doing some shooting related task on most stages. This is especially true in the lower capacity divisions where you are frequently required to reload. That having been said, it is still important to understand how to accomplish movement effectively.

*I like to keep two-hands on the gun when I move.*

The most important thing to understand about moving on a stage is that you aren't really accomplishing anything except getting to someplace you need to be. Many instructors refer to this as "dead time." This is for good reason. You aren't shooting, therefore, you aren't generating any points. This "dead time" needs to be minimized.

I am not going to tell you how to run; you have been running since childhood. What I can do is explain how to run with a gun.

Generally speaking, you want to keep the gun in some sort of ready position. It is good practice to be ready for the next target, and keeping the gun high is a way to do that. Some people call this their "workspace" or "face box" or something like that. As was discussed in the "Position Entry and Exit" section, you need to start aiming sooner in order to shoot sooner. Keeping the gun near your eye line has you in a good position to raise the gun up to your eye line when you begin a position entry.

Some people differ as to whether they want to keep both hands on the gun or not. This isn't a consideration that will make a big impact on stage time, but it is worth talking about. Most people can run faster and more aggressively if they take a hand off the gun. Of course, to enter a position you will need both hands back on the gun. It doesn't make sense to take a hand off the gun in order to run faster unless there is going to be a little bit of distance involved. Most people prefer to keep two-hands on the gun unless they are going to travel five yards or more.

Personally, I keep two-hands on the gun a lot more than most people. I like to always be getting ready for the next target. This is a mindset issue. I want my gun ready for action at all times. It is more important to me to be ready for the next position than to have the sensation of speed that comes with taking a hand off the gun and pumping my arm up and down as I run. In time testing, I have seen that this really is more of a sensation of speed than actual speed.

## From Dave Sevigny (Multiple USPSA and IDPA National Champion as well as IPSC World Champion)

*In most cases, if the move is one or two steps it is best to keep a two-handed grip on the pistol. For any more distance than two steps to the next shooting position, the support hand comes off the grip for better acceleration. When doing a magazine change, try to have it done early so you can fly! When I practice these positional skills, my goal is to feel ready to shoot, even if one foot is all that is touching the ground.*

*Dave Sevigny.*

When moving laterally in the direction of your non-dominant side, it is best to rotate your wrist 90 degrees counterclockwise and point the gun downrange. This should help you avoid issues with the 180-degree safety angle.

*Uprange movement can be done like this.*

Uprange movement is potentially tricky. When running uprange, you need to be extremely cautious of the 180-degree line. Moving uprange, but at an angle toward your dominant side, is easiest. You can simply angle the gun a bit more downrange and move normally. When moving directly uprange, you will probably be quickest if you flip the gun over (by rolling your wrist as close to 180 degrees as you can). With your wrist rolled over, you will be able to run directly uprange with the gun pointed directly downrange behind you. The gun will actually be behind your body using this technique. If you happen to be moving uprange at an angle toward your non-dominant side, you need to keep your wrist rolled so you can point the gun downrange.

In any event, it is important and necessary to put some thought into how you are going to "run with a gun." You need to be confident and safe no matter what direction you are moving. These skills need to be practiced just like any other.

# SHOOTING WHILE MOVING

It is occasionally desirable and maybe even essential to shoot while moving. This presents some interesting challenges compared to static shooting, but the opportunities for improved stage times make it worth looking at.

Shooting on-the-move fundamentally isn't any different than just shooting; the important thing is to remember that all of the normal shooting stance guidelines apply. You need a forward weight bias for recoil control. It is best to be squared up to the targets. If you keep your knees bent, you will be stable. The most important aid is having your knees bent. It is absolutely essential to do this while shooting on-the-move. You need to develop the ability to use your knees as shock absorbers in order to get center hits consistently. This is easily developed during dry-fire training. You simply move about your house and aim at some targets on the wall while working to keep your sight picture as stable as possible.

It should be obvious that the faster you move, the more unstable your sight picture becomes. It is critical to understand that relationship, and to know how fast you can move while still hitting various targets. It is important because you need to know the point at which it becomes impossible for you to consistently hit your intended target.

173

*Bent knees help when moving.*

Shooting on-the-move techniques will change depending on the direction of movement. When moving directly toward or away from the targets you are engaging, you can simply do a heel to toe "roll step." This offers the most stability. If the targets are relatively easy, it may be possible for you to get center hits at nearly a flat run. If you are able to do this (and you should certainly try), then you should employ that technique when possible.

Some people have the idea that they should time their shots so their footfalls do not disturb the sight picture when the shot is actually being fired. This is a seemingly sensible idea, but in practical terms, it is extremely difficult to pull off. It is far simpler to learn how to do a stable roll step. You can intuitively learn to control your sight picture using that technique. Interestingly enough, if you learn to shoot while moving simply based on what the sight picture is telling you, then you may well not shoot when your feet hit the ground. However, that develops organically and isn't forced through some sort of training regimen.

Some other shooters believe that the gun should be brought closer in toward their face when shooting on-the-move. This will keep the gun from bouncing around quite as much while moving, but it will also disrupt the normal upper body triangle position, as well as change the distance from the sights to the eyes. I personally never pull my arms in to stabilize while shooting on-the-move, but with a dot gun, I can see some possible advantage. Experimenting with this for yourself isn't a bad idea, but don't expect any big gains.

When moving laterally, relative to the targets, things get a little bit more complicated. For close range targets, it is no problem to simply twist your torso to engage the targets laterally while you continue a heel to toe "roll step." As you should know, it is easiest to engage targets that are directly in front of you. When the targets are close, this isn't very important. It becomes progressively more important as the distance to the targets increases. The further the targets are, and the more you twist your body to get on target, the more difficult the shooting will be.

It is also possible (if you only need to move a step or two) to do a "drag step." With a drag step, you can stretch out and step far with the foot that is nearest to your destination. You then drag your trailing foot along the ground. Using this technique, you don't actually need to fire any shots while your feet are stepping up and off the ground. The downside is that you can't move very far or very fast while drag stepping.

When moving longer distances, you can "cross step." Using this method, you keep your toes pointed directly at the targets, but step your feet past one another as you move. If you try this in dry-fire, you will notice that it is certainly easy to get your feet twisted up. This requires practice, but it is a very workable technique.

In terms of common mistakes made regarding shooting on-the-move, there are a couple of important ones to talk about.

First, many shooters don't aim hard enough when shooting on-the-move. Simply put, you need to think of every shot as just being tougher when you are moving, because it is! Shoot a 5-yard target like it is a 10-yard target. Aim carefully! Many shooters expect to be just as fast and accurate on-the-move as they are when standing still. This simply isn't the case.

Another mistake is to not move aggressively enough. It is very common for shooters to tiptoe around a stage moving extremely slow. This doesn't reduce the stage time any, but it does make the shooting more difficult. If you are going to move, then move. If you aren't moving at an aggressive pace, then you are usually better off just standing and shooting. Assuming you can effectively shoot while moving, you need to understand when it offers an advantage. It doesn't usually make sense to tiptoe around a stage, even if you are shooting the whole time. Some experimentation is required on your part for you to understand when shooting while moving offers a real advantage and when it doesn't.

At the end of the day, shooting while moving will probably come down to deciding when to do it. You can easily cut your stage times down by shooting on-the-move, but the difficulty and risk level is increased. The best plan is to figure out during practice how fast you can move and still score center hits. Once you have this information, you can go to a match and pace off the targets to know whether you can make the shot or not. Be sure to pace off targets during your training, and you will know what you are capable of.

It may seem silly to some to have a "rule" that you adhere to, but it is a good idea. Figuring this out in the low pressure environment of a practice range is much easier than in a match environment. It allows you to make a dispassionate decision about what your capabilities actually are.

In a match, you may find yourself in a situation where your competitors all seem to be taking a stage on-the-move, and you just aren't comfortable with it. If you know it is outside your current capability level, you are able to stop yourself from getting sucked into trying to shoot above that level. Making these decisions before you even show up at a match puts you in a position to be able to focus on other things.

## From JJ Racaza (USPSA Grand Master, Two-Time World Speed Shooting Champion)

### Shooting while Moving

*Shooting while moving is one of the most important skills that must be learned for any type of shooting—tactical or competition. This is really the only skill set that can be classified as advanced shooting. All other "advanced" firearms skill sets are just basic fundamentals applied in*

*a more efficient manner. In order to successfully shoot accurately while moving, you must lower your center of gravity by bending at the knee, which will allow you to utilize a rolling motion of your foot, which is otherwise known as the heel to toe technique. By lowering yourself to this position, you are essentially separating your body into two halves; upper body and lower body. Upper body essentially remains as stable as can be while the lower body is where you generate smooth and steady movement. Although you may never achieve a completely steady platform for shooting, if done correctly, the movement of your body in relation to your sights and gun can at least be predictable and controllable enough for you to make an accurate shot on target. With time and practice, anyone and everyone can perform shooting while moving consistently. The question is when to use a fast sprint, stop, and then shoot an array of targets, or when to shoot that same array of targets on-the-move . . . Only you know the answer. Comfort level and level of skills all come to play here. One thing is for sure, if you are not comfortable with what you are about to execute, the results will not be in your favor.*

# BLENDING TECHNIQUE

I hope at this point you have a broad understanding of the basic theory of getting in and out of position and shooting while moving. Theory is one thing, but in practice, you are going to find that you will constantly be thrown into scenarios that aren't quite like something you have trained for. You need to be able to adapt to a plethora of different situations.

For example, if a stage starts at a position with a few targets in it, and half a step away you have another target hidden behind some barrels, you can conceptualize your approach to that stage section in a few different ways.

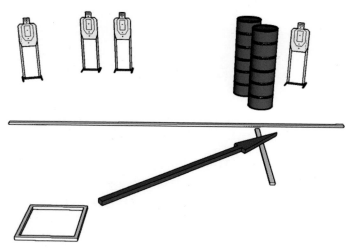

*This is a plausible scenario for a USPSA stage.*

You may see it as doing normal static shooting, then taking a step to another position, then engaging the target behind the barrels, and then leaving that position with the position exit technique described earlier in the book.

You may see that same scenario as shooting static, doing a position exit, and then shooting the target behind the barrels on-the-move.

You may view it as shooting a static position, and then doing the "exit" technique on the target behind the barrels, on your way out of that location.

The important thing to understand with all of those possibilities is that they are all correct. They are correct in the sense that you employ those specific techniques that I described earlier, and you employ them in that specific order. The interesting thing is that all of those concepts get you to pretty much the same place in terms of score.

Some people may resist the idea that all these concepts would produce a fairly even score. I have tested ideas like this, and so have many top level shooters. There usually isn't much of a difference between varying conceptualizations in little scenarios like the example I have shown here. This sport comes down to execution, not stage tactics.

I think the best thing you can take away from this is to find the simplest way to conceptualize a stage and treat it that way. If you have a bunch of targets that appear and disappear, and it is hard to figure out what targets are shot from what position, then maybe the easiest thing to do is just shoot while moving through the whole thing. If you can find some way to relate the scenario in question to the training you have done, you can make it feel familiar and you will have a good method for addressing that stage.

The point of this section is that when you actually walk up to a stage and look at it, the techniques you use may not fit neatly into some little box that I can easily describe in a book. Sometimes a specific shooting scenario is neither fish nor fowl, but requires you to pull the most important ideas from different parts of various techniques and apply them to the circumstances as best you can on that day. To a large extent, that is the tremendous appeal of practical shooting for many people. It is never really the same thing twice.

# TARGET
# ARRANGEMENTS

In USPSA, there are only two types of targets (paper and steel), so it may seem strange to devote so much space in a book to dealing with different targets. The reason that different targets become complicated is that there are so many different ways to arrange them using hardcover, softcover, no-shoots, and so forth.

Before I discuss specific types of targets, I want to specifically define the two main factors that help to determine how to handle the targets.

**Difficulty**
The difficulty of a target is just what most people would intuitively think I am referring to. This is how hard it is to apply marksmanship fundamentals and hit the "A" zone of the intended target. Most everyone would agree that a five-yard USPSA metric target is extremely easy. You can do all sorts of things wrong and still comfortably hit the "A" zone. On the other hand, a 50-yard mini popper is quite a pain in the rear end. Most shooters in USPSA can't hit a 50-yard mini popper with most of the rounds they fire, even with no time limit. Hitting it at speed and under pressure? Forget about it!

## Risk

Risk, on the other hand, is the bad stuff that can happen if you make a mistake on a particular target. For example, if there is a no-shoot target behind a popper, it dramatically increases the risk level of that shot. The shot on the popper itself doesn't become any more difficult, but it certainly adds a bit of pucker factor.

It is important for shooters to understand that risk and difficulty are separate concepts, and they need to be treated separately.

## Open Targets

The most common type of target is a regular "metric" or "classic" target. These targets are relatively simple. You normally just aim at the center of the alpha and let it rip. These targets tend to be very low risk and low difficulty. There isn't a good reason to have a "miss" or even a "D" hit on an open target. The distance needs to be extreme or there needs to be some sort of special circumstance in order for a "D" to be an acceptable hit.

The accuracy standard that I use and teach is to shoot at a pace where you get all "A" hits and close "C" hits. Obviously, anything else is usually considered a mistake. Another good way of thinking about it is that when you are shooting a stage, you are going to make at least an attempt to hit every "A" zone. You don't need to shoot so deliberately as to guarantee an "A." As a matter of fact, guaranteeing "A" hits would be too slow, but every round you fire should be a good faith effort to hit an "A."

If anything, wide-open targets tempt people to rush. It is extremely common to drop points or even have misses on close range targets when you don't aim. It may sound silly to point out that people miss because they don't aim, but it is the truth. When the targets get easy enough, eventually people don't pay them any respect at all. You may not need a perfectly clear sight picture to hit the center of a close target, but you need to aim somehow.

Typically, the misses that happen on open and close targets tend to be transition related. That is to say that people get on the trigger before the gun gets to the target or they pull the gun off the target a bit before they actually fire the second shot on it and they end up picking up a miss.

*I have suffered from many misses over the years on wide-open close range targets. This usually happens during an activator sequence (more on those later). In major matches, I would often have a miss on an open target and not know why. Reviewing footage of the stage in slow motion was how I figured out what I was doing wrong. Once I was aware of the problem, it was clear that it would take a lot of training to fix it. I have spent years trying to become a more disciplined shooter. At major matches, I often find myself fighting the temptation to rush because I know the problems it can cause. The key thing: keep your eyes on a target until you are done shooting it!*

## Partial Targets
Partial targets are any target that is somehow obscured or reduced by some object blocking it.

There are two major schools of thought on how to handle partial targets. The easiest advice is just to aim at the center of the available brown and hammer down. It is simple, it doesn't require much thought, and it works pretty well.

The system I use is much more complicated, but I do believe it results in better hit factors. I think I prefer the more complicated method because shooting minor (as Production shooters do) you just get eaten alive, and all the points down that "center of brown" isn't usually the way to go.

What I prefer is to draw a line (an imaginary line, not a real line) on the target from the center of the available "A" zone to the center of the brown, and then pick a point on that line that I will engage. There are a few factors that help me decide where to aim, and I will break them out below.

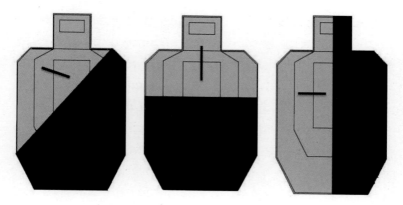

*Your aiming point should be somewhere along the black line.*

You can select the exact aiming point by weighing the following factors:

1. Your skill level.
2. The distance of the target.

3.  Whether you plan to shoot the target while moving.
4.  If you are scoring "major" or "minor."
5.  The probable hit factor on the stage (this one gets complicated).

That isn't an inclusive list, but it should be enough to get you thinking about the possibilities. Essentially, you need to think about how much risk you want to accept. If you are risk averse, then shoot for the center of the brown. If you feel you need the points, and the target is close enough, go for the center of the "A" zone. If you have a sliver of "A" at 10 yards, you may want to aim at the "A"/"C" line.

Let me give you an example to help explain things a bit more. Suppose you are shooting Limited Division (major, obviously, since you aren't an idiot). You have before you an 18 round stage. It will require about two steps of movement. The top guys are shooting it in about six seconds. There is one partial target on the stage, perhaps 15 yards back, and you get a third of the "A" zone. In this situation, the obvious call is to shoot the center of the brown and call it a day. It doesn't make sense to get hard on the sights and try to punch two alphas on the partial target. You will probably not drive your hit factor up even if you get the alphas. (This is Number 5 above; like I said, it can get complicated.)

If you flip the script around, imagine that the stage, instead of being all open targets except for one, is all partial targets except for one. You are shooting Production Division, and you (obviously) will need to do a reload. In this situation, with all the partial targets slowing the stage down (and dragging the hit factor down), and the reload slowing things down, you may well be better served adding a hair more time to the clock and picking more aggressive aiming points on the targets to try and score more alphas.

Are you confused yet? The key to figuring this stuff out is experimenting for yourself. You need to go the range with a timer and a calculator and start figuring out hit factors. Don't just look at the timer, compute the score. You may be surprised.

It also should be pointed out that simply aiming for the head is another option and perhaps a really good one on certain partial target arrangements. You are most commonly going to do this when you have a target that gives you a hair of lower "A" zone because of a no-shoot blocking it, but you get the entire head. Usually, you can just aim for the head and have about an equal probability of hitting an "A," but sidestep the no-shoot.

On the subject of no-shoots, they are generally the highest risk type of partial target. Obviously, they can cost you 25 points in a big hurry with just one misplaced bullet (10 for the miss, 10 for the penalty, and 5 for the "A" you didn't get).

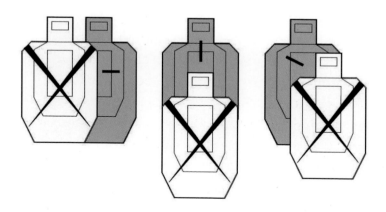

*No-shoots make stages higher risk. I live in fear of hitting no-shoots.*

I can't even tell you how critical no-shoots can be in determining who wins a match and who doesn't. In 2015, at USPSA Production Nationals, the Match Director went nuts with the partial targets. Apparently, the other Division's Nationals were just as bad, if not worse. Since the sport has so many talented competitors challenging for the titles, I think the Match Directors are turning to no-shoots to help sort out who the best shooters are. Don't get caught with your pants down on these. Be sure you train for them.

## Hard Cover

Hard cover, on the other hand, is a serious problem, but doesn't have quite the risk level that no-shoot targets have. The same rule of thumb for selecting an aim point applies, it just isn't as high of a risk.

It is important to point out that it is common to see hardcover both painted on targets and naturally part of a stage. Hardcover that is painted on the targets is much more straightforward than the three-dimensional stuff that you sometimes see.

I usually think of 3D hardcover as "natural" hardcover. If the Match Director wants to force you to a certain position, then you may not get a complete view of the target until you get to that position. There is a wall, barrel, or something else in the way.

The problem is that you can usually see some of the target before you are completely in that position. It isn't binary. It isn't. You can see the target or you can't. It comes down to gradations.

If I had to pick a bone with USPSA shooters generally, I would say they don't have near enough respect for scenarios like this. Too often, I see people head over to a corner of a stage to grab a target that is peeking out from a wall only to stop a bit short and make the shot three times harder than it needed to be. Don't be that dude.

## Soft Cover

Soft cover is a rare challenge. It simply is some obstruction between you and a target, which you are allowed to shoot through. Although this is uncommon, it can be seriously challenging. Essentially, you just need to ignore the obstruction and shoot this target just as if it is an open target. This requires that you know the dimensions of the targets at sort of an instinctual level.

Most of the time, when I have seen soft cover at a USPSA match, it isn't something that the Match Director intended. I have seen stages where it is stipulated that barrels are soft cover (for ease of scoring), and competitors end up blasting the snot out of the barrels, making them actually function as soft cover. I have seen branches and shrubbery treated as soft cover at USPSA matches. Even when these objects are officially treated as soft cover, they may not be that soft. Bullets may well be stopped by them. The point is, if you aren't sure that your bullet will actually pass through the soft cover, then don't try to shoot through it.

## Steel Targets

Steel targets like poppers and plates are a common challenge. They pose all sorts of little particular challenges that all need to be addressed.

First, steel targets are (obviously) smaller than cardboard targets. While this shouldn't be that big of a deal, it is.

The reason it shouldn't be a big problem is that steel targets are usually a lot more generous than the "A" zone of a target. Now, if shooters generally thought of the "A" as their target, there wouldn't be so many people that have an issue with steel. That is more of a cultural issue in USPSA, than an actual technique issue, though.

One of the most challenging parts of shooting at steel targets is the audible feedback you get from steel. You might wonder why this is a challenge.

The tough thing about all the audible feedback you get from steel is that it can confuse the situation as often as it can clarify. You might get used to hearing your shots impact the steel targets during your training, but then in a noisy match situation (with people shooting on bays next to you), you may fire a good shot and then be confused because you don't hear the audible feedback. You may hear a hit on steel, and then not have the steel fall, because it was actually an edge hit. You may hit some other object (like a metal target base), hear the hit, and think you hit the steel target.

The steel does fall when you hit it, but it can take a couple of seconds for that to happen. Obviously, you don't have time to sit and wait around for that to happen. A couple of seconds of delay in a position is far too long.

I think the best solution for these problems is to train on a variety of falling steel, non-falling steel, and paper targets. It is the best way to get used to what you will be seeing and hearing. I do not personally use, or recommend using, "active" hearing protection while actually shooting stages, largely because of the steel issue. I don't want to rely on my ears and don't want to be distracted by what I am hearing. It is also nice not being able to hear people's irrelevant side conversations behind me.

Another challenge with steel is that often you will (for various reasons) end up shooting a steel target last as you leave a position. It is important to recognize that although this doesn't increase the difficulty of a steel target to shoot it in this way, it will increase the risk. Should you miss the steel target and commit to leaving the position, you will waste all sorts of time in order to re-engage the target. (I call this the popper dance.) It is important to dial a little bit of extra certainty into your plan to address this target during the stage inspection period. What I mean by that is to select an aiming method that will get you the hit that you need more reliably than you otherwise might.

Steel targets that activate moving targets or other props are also risky. It is common practice to see steel activate different targets, and more advanced shooters tend to run a whole sequence of targets in a very particular way. I will address moving targets and those target sequences in more detail in the next section, but the important thing to recognize here is that activator steel does have an element of risk to it. Firing a miss on it can carry more of a penalty than just an extra shot. You might think you hit an activator steel, and then shoot a whole sequence of targets only to realize the moving target isn't where it should be because you missed the activator. This is a bad day!

At this point, it should be clear that there is a plethora of different targets in USPSA. You can spend countless hours training a specific target at a variety of ranges and learning the ins and outs of each target presentation. However, that isn't enough! You need to be able to seamlessly transition from one target type to another without a pause. You need to walk through a stage and know the best way to handle the target presentations without a whole lot of deliberation. It can take years of training and experimentation to figure this out. Even then, you will show up at a match and occasionally see things you haven't seen before.

# ACTIVATORS AND MOVING TARGETS

The discussion of target types would be woefully incomplete without some special attention paid to moving targets and the complicated target sequences that go along with them. This includes things like swingers and drop turners. I also include Max Trap targets in this section, even though technically the target doesn't move. There are two main things that you need to understand in this section. First, there is the shooting mechanics when it comes to the targets themselves. Things like how to track a swinging target and how to pick the right aiming point are critical questions. Aside from just the raw mechanics, you need to understand how to sequence targets properly. I have organized this section so the target types and shooting mechanics are discussed first, followed by a discussion of sequencing the targets.

## Swingers

Swinging targets are one of the more common moving targets that you will encounter at a match. It is just a target setup with a counterweight that will force it to swing on an axis. I firmly believe that if you can master shooting a swinger in all of its configurations (there are a few), then you can handle shooting any kind of moving target.

If you are new to shooting USPSA, you have probably seen a swinging target and been really freaked out by it. Most people go through a phase where they squirt as many bullets as they can at a swinging target as it comes into view, and then they move on. The points they score on the target are a crapshoot. People I see doing that are usually pretty happy if they get two hits on the cardboard. If you start training a little bit and applying the right techniques, you can turn two hits anywhere on the brown into two probable center hits.

Commonly, a swinger is available at the end of its swinging arc. The swinger stops briefly as it changes directions (the direction change is called the "dwell"). Obviously, you are going to be shooting the swinger at the dwell if at all possible.

Generally, I see newer shooters put the gun where the swinger will dwell and get on the sights. When they see brown flash behind the sights, they start blasting. When the swinger goes away, they either stay on it for another pass or try to look at their holes on the swinger to make sure they hit it. This is all bad stuff!

What you should do is place your gun where the swinger will dwell, and then start looking to the swinger. When the swinger comes out from behind cover, you should bring the gun to the swinger and "track" it. You move the gun with the swinger to the dwell point, and then away from the dwell as you shoot the swinger. Each shot is aimed. Each shot is deliberate.

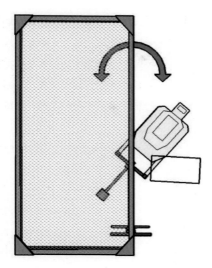

*Bring your gun to the "dwell" spot.*

You should target focus on the swinger instead of on your sights. This applies even if the swinger is a bit further away than you would normally be comfortable shooting while target focused. I have found people are more successful while shooting moving targets if they follow the target with their eyes and shoot from a blurry sight picture.

In addition, it is critical you move the gun with the moving target. You must keep the gun on the target. Stopping the gun to shoot means you are behind.

In terms of pace, don't panic or rush. Just shoot! You need to aim each shot you fire on a moving target the same as you need to aim on any other target. If you don't know where you are hitting, then you probably aren't hitting where you want to!

Almost everyone, B class shooter and up, can get two center hits on a regular swinger, like this, in just one pass. If you are very new or slow at shooting, then you may need to take one shot per pass in order to get your hits on the swinger. Make that decision before you start shooting the stage!

You may have a swinger that is not available during the dwell, but instead can only be seen when it is moving at full speed. These targets can be seen be through windows or over barrel stacks.

These targets are a bit tougher to deal with, but still should present no problem.

Instead of engaging the target where it "dwells," you should be planning to engage the swinger opposite of where it appears. So, if it is going to come out of the left side of a wall, then you wait over on the right to shoot before it goes back behind cover. This can get complicated. The swinger is going to keep switching which side it will appear from, so your stage plan needs to include figuring out when you will be shooting that swinger, and planning accordingly.

You should also work out (based on your prior experience) how many shots per pass you will shoot on a "top only" swinger. It is not uncommon at big matches to have these targets moving fast enough that the top guys can get only one shot per pass on them, so be prepared to swallow your pride and shoot more passes on them.

The important rule to remember for the "top only" swingers is that you should be tracking the target in a straight line.

The targets move in a little bit of an arc, sure, but if you ignore that arc and just work on a straight line, you will have an easier time following the swinger and not have to worry about any vertical movement with your gun.

Let me emphasize the biggest problems I see with swingers.

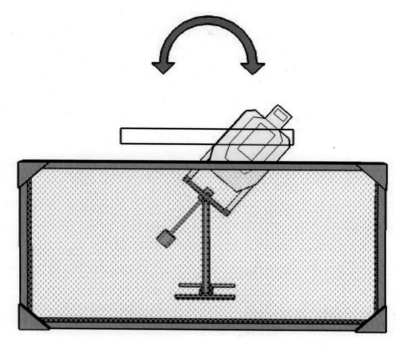

*Track "top only" swinger in a straight line.*

Rule number one on swingers is: Don't panic. Don't spray bullets. You absolutely need to aim your shots when you shoot at swingers. I know I mentioned this before, and I know it sounds crazy, but this seriously is a common issue on swingers. The problem is that spraying bullets on swingers works sometimes. It really does! Sometimes, you spray bullets at them, and you get good hits. You then figure that's the way to do it! I have seen it happen (and done it myself), so I understand the mentality at play here. If this is you, then believe me, you can change. You can aim. There is time! You just need to try.

The second most common issue I see is that people tend to hit toward the bottom of the swinging targets. Just to be clear, I mean the bottom of the target, if the target was set vertically (just like you usually see targets). It is extremely common to see many holes on swingers in the lower "C" and "D" zone, especially at the local match level. Although I can't prove it, I suspect that the lower part of the target draws people's eyes to it, because it is moving the slowest. Since USPSA shooters train to look to a spot and have the sights show up there, it is easy to see why their shots would hit where they look.

The best solution to the swinger problem is (surprise) to get your hands on a swinging target, if only for an afternoon. Make friends with your local Match Director and ask him to lend you the swinger, or train on it a while after a match. All you need to do is prove to yourself that there is, in fact, plenty of time to aim. As soon as you know you can hit swingers in the center, then a lot of the anxiety associated with them goes away.

## Runners

Running targets (sometimes called sliders) are targets that move in a straight line. These targets are usually set up so they move perpendicular to the shooter (laterally). They aren't usually constructed so they move directly toward or away from the shooter, but that is a possibility. The following discussion only applies for the runners that move laterally. Targets that slide directly toward or away from you should be treated like drop turners (covered later).

Running targets are a rare occurrence. Since they are so uncommon, they can be intimidating for many shooters.

With this type of mover, the biggest consideration comes down to figuring out how much time you have to engage the target. When you see the target move during the stage inspection time, you will get a good idea of how much time you have to shoot the target. Running targets are sometimes disappearing targets, so there may not be any penalty with shooting a miss on them. It is essential to figure out if the mover is scored as disappearing, so you know whether it is advantageous to engage it at all.

The way to shoot a mover is to simply line up the sights on it and shoot. You should keep the gun moving, tracking the moving target during engagement. Don't try to "ambush" the mover, that technique will make it tough to score center hits. As long as you keep the gun tracking the mover, it shouldn't be too difficult to engage the target successfully.

One consideration that can exist for running targets is how much to "lead" them. Depending on the distance to the runner, this can be an important factor. If the runner is far away and moving quickly, you (theoretically) may have to aim in front of the target to hit it. In practice, runners usually aren't that far away or moving all that fast. Also, unless you are a physics whiz, or very experienced at shooting these targets, you will not know how much to lead the target. What I would advise you to do is to aim for the center of the mover unless you are absolutely certain that you need to lead it. You can discuss this with other shooters on your squad and see how their hits are working out. If you are up first, that may not be an option. Just remember, unless you are sure you need to lead the target, I wouldn't mess around with it. Shooters routinely overestimate the lead required and get bullets in front of the target.

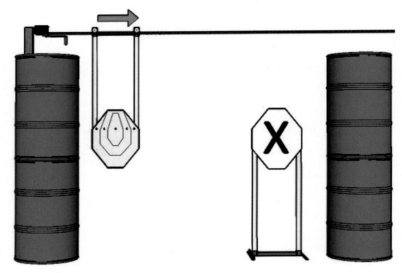

*"Track" the target. Keep your gun moving.*

## Activator Sequence

An activator sequence (for those that find the term confusing) is when a moving target is activated somehow, then you perform some other actions, and then you shoot the moving target. A common example of this would be shooting a popper that activates a swinger, then shooting a static target, and then shooting the swinger. This is the most common scenario, but there are many others.

Shooters typically have all sorts of questions about activator sequences. How do I shoot the swinger? How many other targets do I shoot? And so forth. First, I am going to address the questions about how to handle the activator sequence.

The most important question, in terms of strategy, is figuring out the actual sequence that you are going to shoot the targets in. Should you shoot two static targets before you engage the swinger or only one? Every scenario is different, and it is tough for many people to figure out how to address them. The way to figure these sequences out is to determine the answer to two questions:

How much time is there between activating a target (usually shooting a popper) and the target being in a position for you to actually engage it? Is it a second? Is it two seconds? You don't need to know exactly, but you do need to have a fairly concrete idea.

With the time you have between activating the moving target and engaging it, what can you do? Can you shoot one target? Can you engage three? Can you move a few steps?

With regard to the time you have between activating a mover and shooting the mover, there are a few things you need to know.

Every mechanism is different. If there is a cable attached to a popper, the amount of slack in that cable will have a big impact on the amount of time it takes before that cable does anything. If the cable is stretched so there is zero slack, the cable will do its thing almost immediately when the popper is struck. If the popper needs to have fallen all the way over before it pulls the cable, then the activation of the prop will be slow.

It is common for newer shooters to activate a swinger, then shoot everything else available, and then come back to the swinging target. The rationale for doing this is to give the swinger time to slow down before engaging it.

The fact is, swingers don't slow down very much in the context of shooting a stage. Try activating a swinger, and then slowly counting to five. You probably (depending on the construction of the swinger) will not see the motion slow appreciably. In any event, if you activate the swinger, and then wait some unspecified amount of time for it to slow, you will not have any idea where the swinger will be located when it comes time to engage it. The truth is, there isn't any way around learning how to "time" swinging targets. You will eventually need to do it if you wish to progress in the sport.

There are a great many little variables, like cable tension, that affect movers and activators. The size of the popper matters. The weight of the moving target matters. The power of the ammunition you are shooting matters. The list is virtually endless. The point of this isn't to make you memorize a list of possible variables. That isn't helpful. What does matter is that you understand that no two moving targets work the same way, so you need to pay attention to how they operate.

The most critical time to pay attention is during the demonstration of the prop. When it is your squad's turn to get a look at the movers, watch them closely. If you see other competitors running the stage before it is your turn to shoot, pay attention to that as well. You need to know how much time there is so you can plan effectively.

Once you know how much time you have, you need to figure out what you can do in that time. Again, every stage is different, but there is one thing you need to understand. On most moving target setups, just about anyone, B class shooter and up, is going to have sufficient time to engage at least one static target between activating the mover and shooting it. If you are at that B class level, and you activate a target and then just wait for it, odds are you are doing it wrong.

This is where this issue gets sticky. If you accept that the mid-level to advanced shooters should have time to shoot some other target, and then go to the mover most of the time, then you are probably wondering how to know when you should be engaging a target or two with the time you have. There isn't a universal answer to this. Each shooter needs to assess and know his or her abilities during practice. It is as simple as that. If you pay attention to what the timer is telling you during your training, you will know how long various actions take you. If you don't know your times, then you are in a tough spot.

If you aren't exactly sure of what you can do in the time you have, it is possible to follow the lead of the other shooters of your approximate ability level. This sort of thing even happens on super squads. No matter what the level of shooters, there is sometimes a bit of uncertainty. In those situations, your best bet is to go with what the pack is doing. You should either do that or choose the more conservative of the various options you are debating.

It is possible to "drive down" a steel popper in order to speed up the activation of a prop. With multiple shots, the popper will fall a little faster. This isn't always the best option, but it is something to keep in mind depending on the scenario. Multiple shots on an activating popper will also help you be certain that the popper will fall. This may sound like a small thing, but in a major match scenario, it is nice to be sure you will drop a critical target.

One concept that has helped me a lot is to think of every activator sequence as "timed fire." Generally, all the shooters at my level fall into the same plan on any given activator sequence. Since we all basically shoot any given scenario the same way, we all end up with the same time. With that being the case, I try to collect all the points I possibly can. From the moment you activate the mover until you engage it, the time is going to be the same if you shoot the same sequence as the other guys. The only thing you can do to make a difference in that time is to shoot better points.

Once you understand how activator sequences work, you need to understand how to apply that knowledge to different types of targets. The following list should cover most of the more common things you will see at matches.

## Disappearing Targets

Some targets are scored as "disappearing targets." Usually these are the targets discussed previously, such as "drop turners," but not always.

You should remember that a target being considered "disappearing" is really just a scoring consideration. If the match officials tell you they are scoring a target as disappearing, that means you aren't required to shoot at it. Of course, that doesn't mean you shouldn't shoot at it. Let me explain.

It is not always to your advantage to shoot a disappearing target. It can add seconds to the stage time. In the end, this becomes a stage breakdown consideration. Do you shoot the drop turner or not? Some important considerations weigh into that decision.

First, you need to know how long it will take to shoot the disappearing target. The answer for this is very much scenario dependent. This comes down to having knowledge of how long it takes to do various actions such as transitioning, split times, etc. This will be addressed in a bit more detail later on, but it very much requires that you pay attention to the timer during your training.

If you know how long it takes to shoot the disappearing target, you then need to know what the hit factor on the stage is likely to be. If the hit factor on the stage is 12, for example, then you know you need to generate more than 12 points per second shooting the disappearing target in order for it to be "worth it" to bother engaging the target.

With those two pieces of information, you should be able to make a decision. However, there are a couple of facts that are commonly overlooked when shooters make these decisions.

First, you shouldn't count on getting all the available points on a disappearing target every time. If there are 10 points to be had on a drop turner, don't think you will always get all 10. This is unrealistic thinking, and it will skew your decision making in favor of shooting that target when perhaps you shouldn't.

Second, if you think the score will end up being a "wash" between shooting the disappearing target and not shooting it, you should skip it. Shooting at the disappearing target when you have nothing to gain doesn't make sense. You are introducing an additional element of risk into the stage, and you don't need that.

If you can't decide whether or not to shoot a disappearing target, don't worry about it. This is one of those instances where you will not go too far wrong by just doing what everyone else is doing. Even if everyone (including you) skips the disappearing target, and the best way to do it was to shoot the disappearing target, then you just end up "level pegging" with the people you are shooting against. No big deal.

# STAGE THEORY

**B**eing a good USPSA shooter is about more than just shooting mechanics. You can have all the speed and accuracy in the world, but if you don't know how to compete, you can't do very well.

To be honest, I am still a little bit amazed that there are shooters who show up to matches and don't bother to have a clue about any of this stuff. Stage tactics, visualization, and mental management are all just as necessary to learn as the shooting part is. I frequently see guys chilling out under the shade smoking a cigarette when they should be walking through a stage and visualizing it. These same guys are surprised when they forget targets or have a couple seconds of hesitation where they figure out what they are supposed to be doing on a stage. If you master these ideas, then you will not be that guy any longer.

Anyway, I have a simple process for how a stage flows from the moment you see the stage until the time you are shooting it.

The process for shooting a stage:

1. Look the stage over
2. Decide how to shoot that stage
3. Program that stage plan
4. Execute the plan

These steps are extremely general, and everyone can agree on them. I want to cover the important parts and clarify a few ideas.

When you first walk up to a stage, you get a sense of what you need to do and formulate a plan for doing it. This may be something really simple, or it could be an extremely complex stage. It all depends on what the Match Director decided to throw at you. This is commonly known as "stage breakdown" or "doping the stage." There is a chapter on this process later in the book.

After making a decision about how to shoot the stage, the stage needs to be "programmed."

"Stage programming" is the term I have decided to use for visualizing the stage or "burning in" the stage plan. This is the technique for taking the conscious decisions made during the walkthrough and stage breakdown phase and getting your brain prepared to execute that plan. You can call it "visualization" or "rehearsal," if you prefer.

So, why is programming the stage so important?

When you shoot a stage, there isn't going to be time to think your way through all the little details of your technique. There absolutely isn't going to be time to be thinking about where the targets are or anything like that. You need to subconsciously know exactly where everything is on the stage and what it is you should be doing. If you need to think about it, you are losing time.

The reason I am calling the visualization process "programming" is that shooters go through a stage and tell their mind what they are about to do. They, in a sense, consciously program themselves to execute a certain stage plan.

There are a few important things that require some clarification.

One interesting thing that needs to be reiterated is that when I say shooters shoot without conscious thought, it isn't true, strictly speaking. Top shooters do have conscious thoughts in their heads while shooting; the thoughts just aren't usually directing the shooting.

For example, a shooter is shooting a stage "running their program," and they notice that a piece of steel they shot is falling slowly. They may have a conscious thought in their head saying, "Oh wow, that steel is falling very slowly." That thought doesn't have anything to do with the program they are subconsciously executing. When shooters do have thoughts that affect their program, it can cause them to make errors. It is common, for example, for shooters to think, "I need to speed up!" after making a mistake. This is almost never a good idea. Going faster to make up for lost time isn't a winning strategy in USPSA. It generally just leads to disaster.

Obviously, on a USPSA stage, you aren't going to have time to think your way through everything and still keep up with the top shooters. For that reason, you need to program your way through that stage so you don't have to think about it!

Shooting a stage without thinking about it probably sounds like a massive task to someone that can't do it. You shouldn't be intimidated, though. When someone is new and still learning many new things, they necessarily need to think their way through all sorts of techniques. You need to think about the index point on the gun when you draw, how the trigger should feel like it is going straight back in to the frame, and a whole list of other things. During your training, you can work on any individual skill by itself. You can think about it all you want. There is no better way to learn. Isolate the thing you want to improve and work on it by itself. Once you get that thing to the point that you don't need to think about it any longer in order to execute it, then move on to the next thing.

Stage programming is essentially calling on yourself to perform all those little tasks that you worked on during your training. Draw here, shoot that, let the sights settle on that, transition over there, reload here, etc. You need to step back and let the stage happen without consciously trying to get in the way of the process.

One interesting phenomenon to point out is that the top shooters in the game are usually not a whole lot better at the techniques listed in this book, not in an easily tangible sense. If the best guys in the world can do a draw in .7 seconds, then lots of people can do them in the .8 seconds or so. There isn't much of a gap when you look at skills in isolation from one another. What makes top shooters, the top shooters, is that they can hit a fast draw time at the start of a complicated stage without thinking about it. The lower level guys can only hit a really blazing draw time on the practice range when they don't have to string a bunch of techniques together with it.

The important thing to take from this is that you need to understand what the goal of the technical stuff is. The point is to learn it well enough that you don't need to think about it. You can't do well when you need to constantly think "pull the trigger like this" while you are trying to shoot a stage. It all needs to be internalized.

# TRAINING
# YOUR FOCUS

One helpful habit you can develop is the ability to direct your mental focus to different shooting related tasks while shooting a stage. I am going to explain briefly why this is potentially helpful and why it is important. I want to clarify a couple terms, and the way I am using them, so there is no confusion.

Focus is your attention. When I am typing this, my attention is on the message I am attempting to communicate. My body is doing many other things, though. It is digesting food, pumping blood, and breathing. I am hardly conscious of those things unless I direct my focus toward them. Normally, those things just happen automatically. As I focus on the message I am attempting to communicate, my fingers type automatically. I was trained on a keyboard at a fairly early age, and the techniques I learned stuck with me. My fingers always rest on the keyboard in a particular place, and certain fingers hit certain keys. I don't need to think about the technique any longer. Shooting techniques can work in the same way. They happen automatically after you have extensively trained. Practice makes permanent, after all.

In the complicated realm of shooting technique, it is helpful to shift your focus around. You don't do just one task (like typing); you do many different tasks all strung together into a stage. You are shooting one moment, reloading the next, manipulating a prop the next, and so on. Just as having my focus on one particular thing when typing helps me type better, placing your focus on a certain thing will help with different shooting techniques.

If you can accept that having your focus on certain things can help you during shooting, you need to figure out a couple of things:

1.  How do I move my focus around?
2.  What should I focus on?

Almost everyone intuitively understands how to move their attention from one thing to another. The easiest way is to look at the thing you are focusing on. For example, if someone is talking to you, it is considered rude to not look at them. If you aren't looking, they intuitively understand that they do not have your attention. I am certain that many people right now are thinking about how they can have their attention on a few different tasks at once. "Multi-tasking" it is called. This is really an illusion. Just as your eyes can focus on one visual plane at a time, your mind can be in one place at a given instant. This is why people that talk on the phone while driving get distracted (hands-free phone or not). You can either be having a conversation or be driving. People are not good at conscious multitasking.

It makes sense for a shooter looking to train to perform shooting techniques to also train themselves to shift their focus from one thing to another by directing their vision to the thing they are concerned with. I apologize for stating things so vaguely early on, but I want to make sure I leave room in the definition of this for you to be able to apply it broadly. Let me get a bit more specific now.

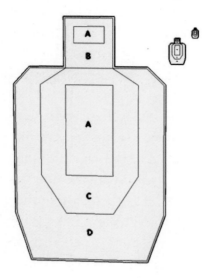

*Targets at 7, 25, and 50 yards.*

I will break down for you a simple little shooting exercise, and then discuss how a shooter would train their attention to be in different places during it. Imagine if you will a series of three targets. One target is at 7 yards, one at 25 yards, and one at 50 yards. The procedure for this little stage is to draw and engage each target with two rounds, then reload, and then engage each target with two more rounds.

For the purposes of this example, I will be selecting various aiming methods for the targets and so on, but understand that those things are not set in stone. The point of this example is to show you how you can train your brain to move its focus around, not to advocate certain aiming methods.

Moving on with the example, let's say on the 7-yard target, you are going to aim using just a flash of your fiber optic sight. You will get a hard front sight focus at 25 yards. You want a hard front sight optical focus at 50 yards, but then you want a mental focus too, on pressing the trigger straight back. Then you are going to reload and repeat.

Think about all the places your mental attention is going to be going. You will look right through the sights on the first close target, and when the fiber is where you want it, you fire. When you see the fiber come back out of recoil, you fire again. You then look to the 25-yard target, find it, and center the sights on it. Your optical focus will shift to the front sight blade, and then the shot breaks. When you see the blade again, where you want it, the next shot should break. You then find the 50-yard target, look to it, and line up the sights on it. The optical focus shifts back to the front sight, then when that is lined up how you like it, your focus shifts to your trigger finger through the press of the trigger. Focus then goes back to the sights to line up the sight picture, and then back again to the trigger. After the second shot breaks, you initiate the reload and direct your attention to the magwell until the magazine is seated. Then your vision shifts out to the 7-yard target, and you run the same sequence again.

Notice how the word "attention" and "vision" are nearly synonymous in the above example. The only time your attention was somewhere other than on your vision was for the careful trigger break at the 50-yard target.

The way to train yourself to move your attention around to where you want it is to become aware of where your attention actually is at various times. For example, I have had many students in classes trained to look their magazines into the magwell when they reload. These students have trained themselves (supposedly) to shoot this way, and I will preach the same thing. During static exercises, most students look their mags into their guns as they have been taught. However, when I give that student a little push, they often don't do that any longer. When that student is made to go faster than they are comfortable going or when they are charging full steam through a field course, their attention drifts off the task at hand to someplace else. You can't start shooting again until your gun is loaded, but despite this obvious fact, many students (under pressure) will take their attention off of that task and put it on running faster or on the next target they plan to shoot. The way to fix this problem is to become aware that it is happening, and then in your practice you train yourself to keep your attention where it needs to be. If you are working on 50-yard targets, and you have your attention on the way the trigger feels, you are a lot more likely to hit where you want than if your attention drifts to how your shooting "feels too slow."

Don't misunderstand: The advice to be sure to direct your attention to one thing at a time is often misinterpreted as to DO one thing at a time. That is not what is being discussed here. Your body is naturally going to do many things at a time. The advice to direct your attention (focus) to one thing is just a recognition that you only have the capacity to direct your attention to one thing. So long as you can only put your focus in one place, you may as well put it someplace useful.

In a high-speed adrenaline-fueled environment like shooting a stage, it can be extremely difficult to quiet your conscious mind and let your techniques work for you. As was just discussed in the "Stage Theory" section, certain conscious thoughts can have a negative impact on your shooting. You may have already experienced the moment in a stage where your mind is screaming, "I need to go faster!" and suffered some very negative consequences as a result. It is clear, then, that something needs to be done about this. Training yourself to move your focus to specific places subconsciously can certainly help keep you from letting your conscious thoughts derail your shooting. Think about this.

# STAGE BREAKDOWN

Stage breakdown is the art of looking at a stage and deciding how you are going to shoot it. This is a fascinating topic to many, and certainly many people are reading this book with a particular focus on this issue.

When the first edition of *Practical Pistol* came out, I don't think there was much of a consensus on how to break down a stage. At this point, I can't really say that the system I use and teach has caught on with the greater USPSA/IPSC community, but maybe it is getting a little bit of traction. It is a system that I know works for me and I am sure it can work for other people who care to use it.

Even though there isn't a commonly accepted system of "how to break down a stage," the top guys usually come to the same conclusion on stages at a major match, even if they are not in communication with each other about the "best" way to shoot a particular stage.
The point is, even if there are plenty of ways to conceptualize how to figure out a stage, many people can look at

a stage and draw pretty much the same conclusion on the best way to shoot that stage.

In any event, if you aren't sure how to approach a stage, then I can give you a system, and you can try it out and see if it works for you. There isn't really a substitute for experience, but applying a system to the stages you regularly encounter, and making mistakes occasionally, should be a good teacher for you.

There is one more thing I should address before I really get deep into the stage tactics discussion. As long as you come up with a stage plan that is broadly logical, that is to say, you aren't creating extra shooting positions for yourself, needlessly backtracking, or having insanely complicated target engagement orders, you probably will not see a huge difference in your results between one logical plan and another. At the end of the day, if you can go left or go right on a stage, it usually doesn't really matter which way you go. Things have a way of balancing themselves out at the end. I like to prove this to myself by shooting a stage in the opposite direction than I otherwise would during my training, just to prove to myself that it doesn't make much of a difference which tactic I choose. I am pointing this out so that when you are at a match under real pressure to do well, you don't get wrapped around the axle trying to figure out the absolute "best" way of doing a stage. Usually, just settling on a plan that you are comfortable with and executing it the best you can is the best play.

Anyway, I have my method for breaking down stages below. This isn't the only method that one could use, but it is a method that should produce the "correct" result.

1. Observe the stage and figure out the stage requirements
2. Figure out your path through the stage
3. Identify the options on the stage
4. Make choices regarding those options
5. Adjust your plan for risk

The first step is to get a look at the stage and figure out what is required of you on any given stage. I am using the word "required" in a broad sense. This might be confusing, and I want to be very clear on what I am talking about.

If it is a 20-round stage, then obviously you are required to shoot at least 20 rounds to finish the stage. If the stage starts with your gun in the holster, then obviously you are going to have to draw your gun from the holster at some point before you start shooting. This isn't exactly earth shatteringly complicated stuff, but I want you to think about what the stage requires in the broadest possible sense.

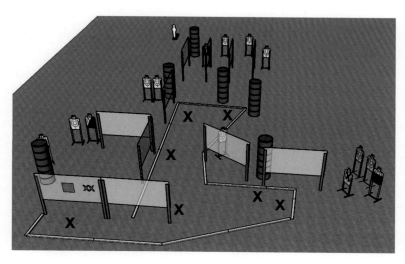

You should also look at where you need to go to on the stage to see all the targets. It might be a 25-round stage, but you are able to see everything from four different places. So, you would be required by the stage to go to all four of those spots in order to see everything.

My point with "requirements" is to figure out, in the broadest sense, where you need to go and what you have to shoot from which location, etc. You don't want to start limiting your thinking this early on in the planning process. It isn't a bad time to start thinking about options. If you see a place where you will probably have a long run between shooting positions, then you might start thinking "that would be a good spot for a reload," but you don't quite want to close yourself off to other possibilities just yet. Again, get a broad sense of where you need to go and what you need to do.

After you get a sense of where you must go in the stage, I like to pick my path through the stage. This means that this is the time where I pick the order of the positions I am going to shoot. Generally speaking, right-handed shooters work best left to right. It is generally easier to move downrange rather than uprange. However, I let the target presentation tell me what I will probably prefer on any particular stage.

Remember that you should always be able to come back to this step. If you are looking at your options a bit further down the planning process and decide you like a different path through the stage better, then by all means switch to that path through the stage and start planning your options that way.

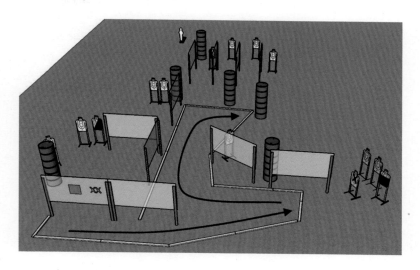

Once you pick your path through the stage, the next part of the process is to identify all of the options on the stage. It is (again) important to make sure that you don't disregard options that you feel are a bad plan yet. You want to keep an open mind for as long as possible! You will probably see other dudes looking at the stage and probably walking it through one way or another. If you are completely clueless about what to do on a stage, it usually isn't a bad idea to copy someone that does have a clue. However, if you aren't overwhelmed by the stage, then watching other people walk through it is probably going to close you off to some possibilities you might otherwise see. If you don't see an option that is available to you, then you can't possibly choose to do that thing.

Just to be crystal clear on this point, the most common mistake when it comes to stage breakdown is to fail to consider an option that you would have otherwise picked. Keep as open a mind as possible and you will see more options.

## Identify all the places where targets are available

It is important early on to figure out all of the places where the targets are available from. I think more often than not, targets are available only from one location, but there will be plenty of targets you can see from multiple shooting locations.

Usually, it is really apparent where I would prefer to shoot a target. I usually like to shoot targets when they are closest or when I am already stopped to shoot a bunch of other targets. However, what you might prefer (all other things being equal) may not be the best way to shoot that particular stage.

## Look for places to shoot while moving

A way to shave time off of a stage is to shoot while moving. On some stages, there may not be good places to do it, and on others the top shooters will shoot the entire stage without stopping. It just depends on the scenario. When initially looking at a stage, find the spots that you are able to shoot while moving. You don't need to decide to do it or not do it at this point, just find the places where it is plausible to shoot while moving. You can make the actual decision about shooting on-the-move later on in the planning process.

## Identify possible "aiming" options

As discussed at length in the "Target Transitions" section, you should identify the targets where you have a choice to make. Maybe you feel like it is a good opportunity to collect all the points on certain targets or maybe you want to play it safe. This is stage dependent, but it is a good thing to think about as you look over the stage.

## Identify strategies for dealing with activators and moving targets

When there are moving targets, almost everyone B class and up is usually going to activate the target, do something else, and then shoot the target they activated. Identify the possibilities for what else you could do (like shoot this target, reload, or whatever). You should keep in mind that there isn't always time to put something between activating a target and shooting that target, so don't feel the need to slavishly adhere to doing it.

If you aren't certain what the "best" order for you is, then you should borrow the plan of another shooter on your squad at a similar level as you. The last thing you need is to have uncertainty working its way in to your brain when you are trying to come up with a plan.

## Identify possible target engagement orders

When walking through a stage, you should get a sense of possible target engagement orders. Look at how the targets present themselves as you move through the stage and get a sense of what the options look like. This is a good time to forget about what your personal preferences are, and just look at the stage for what it is. Sure, you may always prefer to shoot left to right, or whatever, but the targets might lay out in a way that it makes a lot of sense to go the opposite direction. Don't close yourself off to the possibilities.

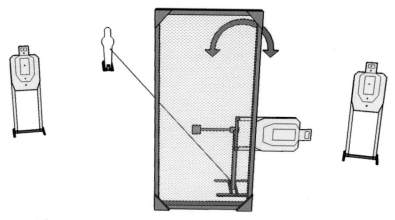

*There are many possible engagement orders in this scenario.*

## Identify good places to reload

In the lower capacity divisions, you will need to reload frequently. When looking over a stage, find the good spots to reload. You want to find all the "good" places to reload. Generally speaking, the more movement you will be doing during the reload, the easier it is to get it done in that time. This isn't a hard and fast rule. You may have quite a distance to run up range or something, and that can make it tough to get the reload done.

After working through all of the available options, it is decision time.

You already have your path through the stage, you broadly know where it is you need to go and what target is being shot from which location. The easiest thing to decide on, then, is the target engagement order. Generally speaking, simple is better. Shooting positions from left to right or right to left is almost always easier than shooting targets in some seemingly random order.

With the position and target order figured out, you don't have a lot left on your plate. I like to ask myself one question at this point in the stage planning process:

"Is there anything cool I can do to save points or time?"

This is where the little details come in, like backing out of a position while shooting at a certain target or shooting on-the-move through a section of the stage. If I see a way to be a little more efficient, and I decide it is worth the effort, then I put that stuff in my plan at this point.

I should point out that I usually figure out reloads at the end of the stage. I see so many shooters get sucked into letting the reloads determine their stage plan instead of the other way around. Sometimes the best way to shoot a stage is to reload after the first target, but if you are letting the reloads drive your decision making, then you probably will never opt to dump a mostly full magazine on the ground even if that is the smartest thing to do at that point.

The final step in the process is to assess the risk level of your plan. Sometimes you will come up with a plan on a stage that you came to in a very logical and reasonable way, but when you look at the plan as a whole it is very risky. You may plan to shoot a complicated 30-round stage with steel and moving targets using exactly 30 rounds. That kind of thing is risky to the point of being crazy.

If you can find a practical way to do it, then leave yourself extra rounds for tough targets or steel. Standing reloads are a really bad thing, so you should set yourself up to minimize the chance of that happening. If you aren't comfortable shooting head shots on-the-move, then don't do it, even if some loudmouth on your squad tries to talk you into it.

When you are thinking about the risk level of your plan, you need to trust your gut. If you don't feel comfortable and confident in your plan, then you might need to get a new plan. For this reason, I personally favor simple plans over plans that are more complicated. I tend to like something that I can aggressively execute more than something I really need to work hard at to bring off.

*Matt Hopkins.*

## From Matt Hopkins (USPSA Grand Master)

*I don't like to worry about minor differences in time between different plans. A stage plan that is a quarter of a second slower than some other option is fine. This sport comes down to execution, not stage planning. The key is*

*to come up with a plan that you are comfortable execut-*
*ing. You don't want to get sucked into shooting a stage*
*the same way as everyone else just because they all do it*
*that way.*

One thing that must be pointed out is that you need to be very careful when it comes to "contingency planning." Contingency planning is the idea that if one thing happens on the stage, then you will do something else as a response. For example, a shooter might say that if they miss the steel over in one position, they will stop in a different place to shoot at it. These plans can get complicated in a big hurry, and most people are not very good at executing them. The reasons for this will become clear in the "Stage Programming" section. The short answer for why contingency planning is generally a bad idea is that effective programming gets you ready to execute a specific plan with zero hesitation. It is difficult to work a conscious decision-making process into that. By "conscious decision-making process," I mean the "Oh S***" response you will have when you make a mistake and need to switch to your new plan. That response usually burns up valuable time.

# TYPES OF STAGES

I often hear terms like "speed shoot" or "field course" thrown around. I use terms like these myself. I think it would be useful to explain what these terms mean for those who don't know. In addition, I want to give you a few little tips for these types of stages. These labels aren't a hard and fast thing. These are broad categories that help people conceptualize the best way to shoot the stage. The categories aren't even mutually exclusive.

**Field Course**

The "field course" is the most common type of stage in USPSA. This type of stage involves multiple positions and lots of targets. These stages can contain all sorts of options or they may be very straightforward.

On these stages, all the movement (during which time you aren't generating any points) tends to drag the hit factor down. At the USPSA nationals, the Production high hit factors on these stages are usually six or seven. Most of the top shooters in the sport put up times on these stages that are within a couple seconds of each other. There are rarely any "breakout" runs where someone puts up a really fast time. If there is, that person usually got a fast time by using a tactic on the stage that other shooters didn't see or decided not to use.

Field courses are the "normal" stages. When I am shooting them, I just try to cruise through and not screw anything up. Since I can't do well simply by going faster than everyone else goes, I just want to shoot these stages with no big mistakes. These stages are the bread and butter of USPSA. To do well, you need to move efficiently and shoot disciplined. There isn't any shortcut around that.

## Short Courses

Short courses are the small stages. They usually require you to stand in one spot. Occasionally, you might need to move a few steps.

The hit factors on short courses tend to be a bit higher than field courses, because there is less moving around.

The shorter the stage, the more "up for grabs" the stage win is. Lower level shooters can swing for the fences on shorter stages, and if they hook up on it, they might win it. I don't get too wrapped up in the individual stage results on the shorter stages for that reason.

## Hoser Stages

Hoser stages consist mostly of really easy shots. These are popular, especially at the club level, but well-designed major matches tend not to have that many of them.

On hoser stages, the times tend to be really close, even more so than other types of stages. These stages simply don't separate people in the results very much. When there aren't hard shots or complicated positions to cause people to make mistakes, it has the effect of bunching everyone up in the results.

Personally, I try to shoot hoser stages under control. Everyone is going to be fast on them, so the only way to get ahead is to shoot as many points as I can. This is easier said than done when all the targets are right up in your face. There is a big difference on these stages between dropping one "C" and dropping six.

Also, since the shots are close, the hit factors tend to be really high on hoser stages. I have seen 32-round stages that have a winning hit factor of over 14! This means that missing a reload or screwing up a draw can have very negative consequences. That's why it is important to not get tense on these stages. When you tense up, you make those mistakes, and those mistakes hurt a lot on hoser stages. That dynamic is made more difficult when you consider that most people really want to rail on hoser stages.

## Mirrored Stages

A "mirrored" stage is a stage that is the same when observed from left to right as it is from right to left. Well, specifically I should say that the diagram and layout makes you think the stage is identical from either side. In truth, no stage is truly mirrored.

I like to keep this in mind when I look at mirrored stages, and I make a real effort to look at stages from both directions. The targets may present themselves very differently if you look at going the other direction. This is something to keep in mind during the stage breakdown phase.

## Speed Shoots

Speed shoots are single position "stand and blasts." The hit factors can be extremely high on these stages! I think of speed shoots as short courses that have moving targets or some other thing that creates a risk/reward scenario.

The term "speed shoot" certainly implies that on these stages it is more important to go fast than it is on other stages. That isn't really true; the scoring system is the same no matter what.

The issue on speed shoot stages is that people (again) tend to get really tense when they are going for a fast time. Missing your draw on these stages will throw you way back in the rankings. Missing your draw is usually due to tensing up.

On speed shoots, there is more of a risk and reward scenario. If you can execute a really aggressive strategy on the stage, you may be able to pick up quite a few points. On the other hand, if you make a mistake you fall way back in the stage rankings. I am not a big advocate of taking a lot of risks, but if you like doing that, speed shoots are a good place to try your luck. (I have heard this called "casino style" shooting.)

## Carnival Stages

"Carnival" stages have many moving targets in them or maybe even some props that people consider to be strange or goofy. There are some clubs that have constructed any number of strange props. There are swinging Texas Stars, roller coaster cars, or maybe even just a slew of swingers you need to engage from one place.

Carnival stages present an interesting challenge. On these stages, the usual scoring considerations can be distorted by the way the props work.

I should explain that more clearly. Normally, I shoot a stage just about as fast as I can go while shooting all "A" hits or close "C" hits. That method will net me the best average hit factors over the course of the entire match.

On a carnival stage, I do things differently than on other stages. When there are lots of moving targets all in one place, it may not be the best to shoot each of the moving targets in such a way that I am sure I will get good hits on all of them. If there are three moving targets that appear, and then disappear in two-second intervals, it may take six seconds to shoot all of them. Think about it. If you shoot one of them cautiously, so you know you got it, then wait for the next one, and then wait for the next one, it could add up to six seconds. It may be more and it may be less, depending on how the targets moved for that run. It can be difficult to predict. If, on the other hand, you were to simply shoot two shots at each target immediately after activating them, when all of them are visible, you may be able to do it in more like two seconds. Even if you left a miss, you would still likely end up with a better overall score because you cut so much time off the stage.

The above example is a little abstract, so let me give you a real one. At a recent major match I attended, they had a stage where you stepped on a pressure pad that activated four swingers simultaneously. A couple of the swingers had no-shoots on them. This slowed their swing down, but made them very tight targets. Almost everyone in the match activated the swingers, and then shot each swinger individually. They would shoot one, then wait for the next, and then shoot it, and so forth. This method produced good hits, but took 8 to 10 seconds total.

I carefully observed the movement of the swingers and came up with an engagement order where I could sling two rounds at each swinger on their first appearance. This was a very aggressive target order, and it would be completed in about three seconds. Even if I had a miss, I would have come out ahead of the conventional method. If I had two misses, I wouldn't be far behind. I shot my plan and got lucky. I got through the stage without any misses, and it obviously worked in my favor.

The best advice I can give on the "carnival" stages is to come up with a plan, and then execute it with zero hesitation. If you take lots of extra time being absolutely certain that you hit everything, you are going to be way too slow. You simply must execute the most aggressive plan that you think you will have a good chance of success on. It will cut seconds off the stage and will usually work out in your favor. I should also point out that I see shooters spend lots of time being certain of all their hits on these stages and end up with penalties anyway.

## Memory Stages

A memory stage is a stage where it is difficult to remember and execute your stage plan.

Usually, these stages are constructed so that targets appear and disappear, and then appear again as you move through the stage. It can be difficult to figure out which targets you have already engaged.

There is sometimes disagreement over whether or not a specific stage is, in fact, a memory stage. For the purposes of the advice given in this section, use the following rule: If you look over a stage and are having a lot of trouble coming up with a plan because there are targets all over the place and it is confusing, then you should treat that stage like a memory stage.

### Here Is Some Specific Advice for These Stages

Come up with an easy plan to remember. This is the most important thing you can do. Even if there is a plan you think is slightly better in a strictly technical sense, it is usually better to disregard that plan in favor of something that is easier to remember.

Use stage markers to help you remember things (more on those later). If you look at the stage and can determine that you need to shoot every target to the left of the barrel in one position, then do just that. You can run up to a position, find the barrel, and take the targets that you need to take. If you use little markers like that, it makes it much easier to disregard the targets that you don't need to shoot at that time.

If at all possible, walk around the outside of the stage from outside the fault lines. You can frequently get a much clearer idea of how everything is laid out if you leave the confines of the shooting area, and locate the targets that way.

If possible, you can inspect the stage while having a friend locate the targets from outside the fault lines. If the pair of you work together to figure out the stage, you have a much better chance of success.

The key thing on memory stages is to do extra visualizations. As soon as you have a plan, you need to "burn it in" even more solidly than most other stages. It is easy to forget to engage a target on memory stages, and you don't want to be that person.

## Standards

"Standards" are the type of stages that have you just stand there and make tight shots. Usually the standards stages have you at some set distance, and it usually consists of multiple strings of fire. It is common for these stages to test both strong hand only shooting and weak hand only shooting.

These stages are pure tests of shooting skill. There isn't really any specific strategy to it. There is nothing cool you can do to gain points or time. You just need to stand there and shoot. In the final analysis, I suggest you do exactly that. Don't try and go extra fast or enact some master strategy on these stages. That is usually the path to disaster. There isn't any way around it. You need to make the shots as well as you can, and let the time shake out how it is going to shake out.

## Classifiers

Classifiers are the stages that determine your rank on a national level. These stages are usually not terribly difficult or complex, but they do get people to make mistakes.

First, it is important to understand that on a classifier stage like "El Presidente," your overall time on that stage is hugely impacted by your draw and reload speed. How fast you are actually pulling the trigger usually isn't as important. However, on many of the higher hit factor stages, it makes sense to select a slightly faster aiming method than you otherwise would. I tend to eat more "C" zone hits on classifier stages because they are so close and fast.

## El Presidente

3 FT   3 FT   30 FT

*Turn, draw, and engage each target with two rounds. Reload and re-engage with two more rounds. Anything under five seconds is a pretty good time. This is a classic classifier stage.*

# FACTORS IN STAGE PLANNING

I think it is helpful to list some things to think about when it comes to breaking down a stage. This isn't an inclusive list, but it should get you thinking.

## Hit Factor

There are some circumstances where it can be helpful to know the hit factor of a given stage. This isn't a strictly essential thing, as normally you should just shoot the stage at your natural pace and get as many "A"s as you can while doing it. However, there are some times where knowing what the hit factor of the stage will roughly end up being is helpful. You may need to decide if you should skip a disappearing target. There may be a difficult target in the midst of a "hoser" stage, and you decide that you may not want to aim quite as carefully as you otherwise would on this target. If you know that saving some time is worth potentially dropping points, you can get a better score.

## Difficulty

It can be helpful to know if the stage is going to be a difficult stage for the rest of the shooters in the match. With a little experience, you will know how many penalties there are likely to be on any given stage. All of those collective penalties can really swing the match results. If the stage looks really tough, it might be a good idea to adopt a lower risk plan. Taking big risks doesn't make as much sense on a stage that is likely to hugely affect the results anyway. Let the other shooters make mistakes while you cruise the stage without penalties.

## What Sort of Stage Is It?
This was discussed in detail previously, but the idea bears repeating again. Figuring out the "type" of stage may give you some clue as to how to approach the stage.

## Stage Procedure
Understand what the stage procedure is. On some standard exercise type stages, it can be complicated. Read it carefully, and make sure you read it correctly. Clarify any issues you have with the Range Officers on the stage immediately. Some stages that have an extremely simple layout may have a complicated set of instructions to go along with it.

## Target Type
It should be fairly self-evident, but pay attention to the types of targets on the stage. Are there many partial targets? Are the targets close, far, or somewhere in between? The whole point of the stage is to shoot the targets, and it helps to get an idea of what they look like.

## Number of Targets
It should go without saying, but make sure you know how many targets are on the stage. Some stages can be

complicated. It is vitally important to count the targets on these stages and to be sure you don't miss anything.

## Where Are the Targets Available?

This was mentioned previously, but needs to be emphasized. You need to know where all the targets can be shot from. When you look at the stage, look at it carefully. You might be surprised what you see.

## Aiming Methods

Figure out the most efficient method to aim at each target. Are you going to need a hard front sight focus? Can you get away with just seeing the fiber optic rod in the center of the target? Figure out how you are going to address each and every target.

## Construction of the Steel

Take a close look at the steel on the stage. Does it fall forward or backward? Does it look like it is "set heavy" or not? Expecting the steel to react to a hit one way and having it react the other can get in your head during a stage. You don't want any surprises (like trying to "drive down" forward falling steel).

## Construction of the Walls

Walls can be constructed in all sorts of different ways. They may be made of dense material like wood where you can't see through them. The walls may be made of transparent material. Being able to see targets through the walls can change the way you shoot the stage. Pay attention to that.

*Targets can be seen through walls in this example.*

## Construction of the Props

Take a close look at all the props on a stage. How do the doors open? Do you have to twist the knob? Every prop on the stage requires careful examination. You don't want any surprises when you shoot the stage.

## Range Surface

The surface of the range requires some attention at times. It may be wet or muddy, requiring you to be very careful when you move around. The range may be gravel. It may be grass. It may be a mixture of these things. It may seem obvious, but you do need to pay attention to the range surface.

## Positions

You should identify all of the viable shooting positions on any given stage (covered previously).

## Markers

There is a whole section on how to use markers later in the book, but the real trick is remembering to locate them while walking through a stage. Find useful markers and utilize them.

## Targets You Can Move in and Out On

Closer, relatively easy targets can be a great opportunity to shoot while moving. When walking through, you should view those targets as opportunities, and capitalize on them. Having a close target to "set up" on is really helpful.

## Shooting While Moving

There may be whole sections of any given stage that you can take on-the-move. If you see one of these sections and think that it is a good option, then don't hesitate to do it.

## Footprints

Footprints on the ground can tell you a lot. You should get an idea of the most popular route through the stage just by looking at the footprints on the ground. If you come up with a stage plan that involves skipping going to an area where you see a lot of footprints, that may be a good thing, or it may be bad. You may have forgotten a target or come up with a genius way to game the stage. Be sure to figure that out before you shoot.

## From Dave Sevigny (Multiple USPSA and IDPA National Champion as well as IPSC World Champion)

*Dave Sevigny.*

### Positioning

*Be sure when you do land to engage an array, if at all possible, plant where you can pivot without side stepping. It is much faster to transition using your knees and ability to bend than being forced to step and reposition for a wide target within an array.*

### Pasters on Targets

The position of the pasters on targets may offer some hints or reminders. If you see the pasters clumped up on one side or the other of a target, it may be a clue that many people are making the same mistake. Maybe you need to lean really far around a wall to be able to see the "A" zone of a target, and most people are just eating "C"s on it. Take a close look when you see clumps of pasters in strange spots.

### Holes in No-Shoots

If you see lots of holes in no-shoots, be careful. You certainly don't want to put another hole in there. A bunch of white pasters on those no-shoot targets should give you a hint to select a very precise aiming method to avoid penalties.

## Areas Where Lots of Bullets Have Hit

There may be areas of the berm that are chewed up from the bullet impacts. If you are wondering where to put your sights while you wait for a moving target, or something of that nature, look at the berm and see if there is a patch of dirt chewed up. It can be a big help.

## Powder Burns on Walls

Powder burns on the walls will tell you where people are leaning around the walls, or shooting while near the walls. Think of this just like a footprint. You will get a good idea how other people have shot that stage, and you can use that to inform your decisions.

# SAMPLE STAGE BREAKDOWN

I thought it might be useful to do an example stage and walk through the stage breakdown process. Before I get into the specifics of the stage, I just want to make clear that this breakdown will be for USPSA Production Division. This breakdown will also be done for me, not for you or anyone else. Everyone is different, and we shouldn't all shoot every stage the same way. The basic ideas will translate to any division and any person, even if the specific stage plan doesn't.

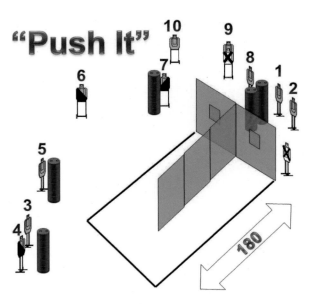

The stage is called "Push It." It is a 20-round stage with all paper targets. There are two "push ports." These ports require you push them open in order to see the targets behind them. The start position is each hand on X marks on the wall. The diagram should more or less clarify the layout of the stage.

As a reminder, here are the basic stage breakdown steps:

1.  Observe the stage and figure out the stage requirements.
2.  Figure out your path through the stage.
3.  Identify the options on the stage.
4.  Make choices regarding those options.
5.  Adjust your plan for risk.

First, we need to figure out the stage requirements. We have 10 targets, 2 rounds minimum fired on each, for a total of 20 rounds. Since the gun is restricted to 10 rounds per magazine, this means we need to reload at least one time. The stage is like a sideways "U" shape. There are push ports with targets behind them, on each end of the "U," forcing you to go to each end. There is also a spot in the middle of the "U" that has a target hidden behind a stack of barrels. Movement-wise, you are required to go to all three of those locations.

The optimal path though the stage appears simple. You have to move from the start position over to the first push port, and then continue moving clockwise around the stage. At some point (or maybe two points), you need to execute a reload. There doesn't appear to be any other path that is a viable option in this case.

With the requirements and the path for the stage determined, it is time to discuss the options. There are a few
of them.

*The view from the start position.*

The first targets (Targets 1 and 2) to be shot on the
stage are both available after opening up a push port.
These are both fairly close and easy targets to hit, but there
is a choice in how to deal with them. They could be shot
from a static position, or they could be shot while moving.
Shooting the targets on-the-move would save a little bit of
time, but it requires you to take them while backing up.
Backing up while shooting is (obviously) a little bit more
difficult than shooting while standing still. However, on
close range targets like this, I think it is more than worth
it for me to shoot the targets while moving, so I don't have
any trouble deciding to shoot these targets while moving.

Notice that Target 1 is partially obscured by some barrels. If you back up a few steps, the target is no longer
visible. For this reason, Target 1 should be shot before
Target 2.

*The view through the first port.*

There is a similar decision to be made in the second
position on the stage. There is a close-range target available as you move into the position, then there is a target
you need to lean around the barrels to get, and then there
is another target you can shoot while moving out of the
position. These are Targets 3, 4, and 5, respectively.

From the photo of Targets 3 and 4, you should notice
the stack of barrels obscuring Target 4. The problem is
that if you move to a position where you can see Target
4, Target 3 is no longer visible. This necessitates shooting
Target 3 while moving to the position from which you can
engage Target 4. There really isn't any other good option
in this situation.

*Approaching the second position.*

After the three targets in that position, there are three more targets available on the way to the end of the stage (Targets 6, 7, and 10). Target 6 and Target 7 are close range partial targets. Target 10 is a 25-yard target. It would be fastest to shoot all these targets while moving, but that doesn't mean it is the best option. At my current skill level, it would be ill advised (to say the least) to attempt to shoot a 25-yard target while moving. It is just not a viable option in this case for me to shoot at Target 10 while moving.

Targets 6 and 7 are a different story. They may be partial targets, but they aren't that far away. It is a bit of a risk to shoot them while moving, but it is worth it. The ability to look at situations like this and comfortably decide to shoot on-the-move is what makes you competitive at big matches.

*Target 10 will be shot last.*

*Target 7 can be shot while moving.*

At the end of the stage, there is a push port revealing two more targets (Targets 8 and 9). Target 9 is partially covered by a no-shoot. So, in the final spot, there are three targets to be shot. Target 10 was skipped before and needs to be dealt with now. The targets revealed by the push port also need to be dealt with. The choice here is whether to start on the close target or the 25-yard target. I tend to prefer to "set up" on the close targets, so I start on Target 8.

*The view from the final port.*

Finally, the other choice to be made is where to reload. It is possible to do one reload on the stage. After shooting five targets, there are a couple steps in which to get a reload done. The other option is to do a reload after the first position and again just before hitting the second push port. That option is workable, but it is an extra reload.

There doesn't seem to be any advantage to loading twice on the stage, so I would opt to do just one.

Finally, I would select an aiming method for each target. Certainly, I want a hard front sight focus and careful trigger presses for the 25-yard target. The rest of them all appear that they can be dealt with using target focus and aiming with the fiber optic dot.

Finally, I like to think about the plan in terms of the risk level. This plan is not terribly risky. The only real element of risk is that I have only one extra round for the entire stage. Any more extra shots than that and it will make a mess of the reloading plan. This doesn't mean the plan will not work, but it is something to recognize. I don't have extra rounds to sling all over the place.

After breaking down the stage, it is time to "program" it, and that is the subject of the next section.

# STAGE PROGRAMMING

Stage programming is the process by which you will "program" a sequence of cues into your memory. Each one of those cues will call for you to execute your shooting skill in some specific way. This is done while you physically walk on a stage and can also be done away from a stage once you have a good knowledge of how the stage looks on the ground. The programming process should be done before you step up to the line to actually shoot the stage.

During your training, you can work on any individual little skill. You work out drawing, reloading, shooting mechanics, transitions, and every other basic skill that a shooter will need. Your training should bring these skills to a level of unconscious competence. This means that you can execute any shooting skill without needing to "think your way through it." When you "program" a stage, you are deciding which skills to use and where to use them.

To a casual observer, this process looks extremely silly. You may see an entire squad of shooters walking around in a line on stages and pointing their arms at targets. Although this may look a bit off, it is the "stage programming" process at work.

Fundamentally, all that you do during stage programming is "visualize" your way through the stage at hand as many times as necessary. That may sound ambiguous to the reader, so I want to clarify a few definitions.

When I say "visualize," I am talking literally about just that. You need to think your way through the stage, and see the stage being shot in your mind's eye. This is best done (initially) by physically walking through the stage and having your body in the positions it will be in when you shoot the stage. You should get your arms pointed at the targets as you would if you were holding a gun, and so forth. Eventually, once you have rehearsed the stage a few times, you should be able to close your eyes to rehearse the stage.

When I say that this needs to be done as many times as necessary, I mean just that. You need to repeat this visualization process, time and time again, until you consciously feel ready to shoot the stage. This could be any number of times. On a complicated stage, it may take a long time to "burn" the stage into your memory. Usually, I will visualize a stage at least 15 times before shooting it. A good rule of thumb here is to program the stage until you can close your eyes and "shoot the stage" in your mind's eye, without any uncertainty about which target is in what position and how you will address that target.

This programming process is an incredibly powerful tool. It is, in fact, a necessary tool if your goal is to do well at major matches. If you have ever observed a newer shooter walk around a stage during the inspection period, you may have a good idea of how important programming is. It is common for new shooters to skip the programming part of shooting because they don't understand how to do it or maybe not even understand what is being done.

These new shooters commonly just walk through the stage and figure out where all the targets are, and then call it done. Consciously knowing the position of the targets and where you plan to reload isn't good enough. You need to be subconsciously ready to execute the stage with zero hesitation or you are behind the curve. That is just a fact of shooting.

### How Fast?

*Some people may wonder how fast they should go through a stage when programming it into their brain. Ideally, it is best if you can program the stage at the speed you will actually shoot it. It can be difficult to run full tilt through a stage when your squad is doing a walkthrough, but, if possible, it is nice to get a feel for the speed you want.*

It is also amazing to watch a shooter walk through a stage and see them make a mistake. If you watch carefully, you will sometimes see a shooter do something silly or just plain wrong while they are visualizing the stage. If you see them do a few repetitions this way, it is almost a certainty that they will make that mistake when they shoot the stage for real. It is amazing how powerful a tool programming is.

If a shooter can program themselves to do something wrong or dumb, it stands to reason that they can program themselves to do something right, as well. If you visualize getting your feet into just the right position to hit all the targets that you want to without moving around, then you will almost certainly execute it properly.

It is important during the programming process to figure out where you are going to put your mental focus, and then visualize putting it there. If you feel that you need to have a crisp sharp sight picture on some 25-yard pieces of steel, you need to visualize doing exactly that. Don't walk through the stage and say, "Oh, I need to aim hard at those." Walk through that stage and imagine exactly the sight picture you want superimposed on those targets. If you program yourself in this fashion, you will almost certainly execute as you have programmed.

Some shooters also find it helpful to imagine the pace of the shooting. This is potentially a helpful thing to think about, yet potentially very dangerous. You may look at the targets and decide that you can shoot them at this pace "Bangbangbangbang . . . " (pause while aiming at a hard shot) "bang . . . bang." If you visualize that pace, and program it in, guess what . . . you are going to shoot that pace, and it may not matter what your sight picture is telling you. This is a valuable training tool, but a potentially match-trashing thing to do. Be careful about this. Some find it helpful, and others can't do it properly. You need to understand your own mental tendencies to know whether this is helpful for you or not.

In any event, you should recognize that programming yourself is a vital and powerful tool. You need to practice doing this properly and recognize that you will perform as you are programmed.

# STAGE MARKERS

If you understand the movement techniques that I described, there is a closely related concept that is really useful. Obviously, you need to be able to find the spot that you wish to shoot from. However, just finding the spot isn't good enough. You need to find it with zero hesitation. You need to find it when match pressure is on. You need to be able to set up to shoot from a position in just the right way, so that you don't unnecessarily shift your feet around. Any mistake will cost you time, so you need a system to avoid these problems.

The most effective tool for finding positions in stages is using a "marker." A marker is just a visual cue. It could be a spot on the wall, a nail in a fault line, anything will do. Some things are certainly better than others. Ideally, the marker that you use should be easily identifiable from the surroundings. Picking a specific rock on the ground is usually a bad idea. It might be tough to find "your" rock when you are shooting a stage at full speed.

There are two primary types of markers. There are markers for where to put your sights and markers for where to put your feet. Fundamentally, these things work similarly. If you understand how to work with both of these types of markers, you should be able to improvise a different type of marker if the need arises.

Markers for your feet are spots on the ground that designate where you want to shoot from. I recommend you pick an extremely specific spot for one of your feet and get that foot to that exact spot. Sometimes the "right" position to shoot from in USPSA can be tiny and hard to get into when you move into it at a flat run. That is why you need a marker to help you find the spot.

When you move to that spot, you need to look at the spot you are headed to until you are sure that you are going hit it correctly. If you don't need to be in that specific of a spot, then you may not need to look at the spot very much at all. If you need to get your foot into an extremely precise position, you may need to look at the marker all the way until your foot actually gets there. It all depends on the circumstance.

*Learning to use stage markers can be difficult. (It certainly was for me.) The natural tendency that most people have is to keep their eyes up on target or looking for targets most of the time. It is difficult for many people to even learn to direct their eyes to their magwell while they reload, or to pull their focus back from the target to the front sight. A big part of this is due to the effects of match pressure (covered at length later). It is important to recognize that directing your eyes around at different things on the stage is counterintuitive and will feel slow at first.*

You can use markers on wall sections or on the backstop to help you find targets. Some targets are hidden behind walls or other vision barriers. Instead of looking for the target, then getting your sights on the target, and then shooting the target, you can instead find a marker to aim at. If you get a marker in the right position, your sights will already be on target when the target becomes visible to you. This can take some practice, but it is a real time saver.

One thing I need to point out is that you are going to need to get into the habit of shifting your vision around a lot. Your eyes often need to go from the sights to the magwell (as you reload), then to a stage marker, then to a target, and then to the sights as you aim at that target. You may move your vision to three or four places in as little as a second. This was covered in greater detail in the "Training Your Focus" section.

# THE "MAKE READY"

After you have trained, showed up at a match, broken down the stage, and programmed the stage, it is time to shoot. I think having a system for handling the "pre stage" routine is tremendously valuable. Some people tend to be way too amped up, and they make stress-induced mistakes. Other guys may be at a familiar club match setting and not have their head in the game because they are too busy chatting with the guys on their squad. In either situation, it helps to have a system.

The first thing you need to do is to monitor your stress level. If you step up to the line and feel good, awesome. If you get up to shoot and alarm bells are ringing in your head, you need to pay attention to them. You may have some indecision about your chosen plan. You may be afraid of the shots you need to make. You may think you are too slow. If the pressure is eating you up, you need to pay attention. Don't ignore it. Manage it.

When the pressure is too much, you need to breathe. Control your breathing. In and out. Nice and slow. Calm yourself. Visualize your stage plan over and over again. Focus on that, and it will bring that stress level down.

If you get up to the line and aren't feeling any pressure at all, you need to do something about that too. If it is a local match, there may not be much pressure present.

A little bit of adrenaline will help you, not hurt you. I (and I don't recommend this for everyone) like to slap myself in the face if I feel I am dragging. Being in 95-degree heat all day can make you tune out of the match. It is time to get back in it! Think about all of the time and preparation you put into this match. Think about some person in particular that you want to beat. Think about your goals. If the stress level is too low, raise it up.

You must develop a routine that you go through at the line. This will give you something to occupy yourself with when you are up there. It will be your last chance to get into the "zone." If you watch a squad of top shooters at a match, you will notice that they all have some sort of routine. They may have different routines, but they all have one.

Let me give you a sample "make ready" routine. Feel free to use it in its entirety, or make up your own.

1. I think the best "make ready" plan starts at the very least when you are "on deck." If you are on a big squad at a major match, you could maybe start it one shooter earlier (when you are "in the hole"). Obviously, you are going to need to know the shooting order to make this work for you, so pay attention! Where you are "in the stack" shouldn't come as a surprise to you. If you aren't sure where you are in the order, ask someone who knows.

2. Once you are "on deck," you should step up near the start of the stage and check your gear one final time. Are your magazines loaded? Do you have Pro

Grip freshly applied? Whatever it is, make sure it is ready.

3. Conversations with shooters around you should stop once you begin prep. If someone comes up and starts chatting you up, just tell them you are up to shoot in a second and you will talk to them after. I try to avoid eye contact with people when I am on deck, so as not to invite conversation.

4. Mentally rehearse the stage over and over again. You should be able to close your eyes and see everything happening in real time/ first person.

5. Generally, it is good to avoid watching the person just before you shoot. It isn't likely that anything you see them do will help you; all it can really do is distract you.

6. After the person before you is done, you get your last chance on the stage to walk through it. Use this time. Walk through the entire stage taking that last opportunity to visualize your way thought it. You should be entirely comfortable with what you are about to do.

7. After you get the "make ready" command, draw your pistol out and get yourself ready. I like to rehearse the start position a couple times at this point. If I am picking the gun up off a table, I do that a couple times to get myself in the zone. If the gun is coming out of the holster, I rehearse that. Whatever the situation, I get comfortable with it.

8. Load your gun and assume the start position.

As I said, the above is just a sample, but as you can see, it is a detailed process of visualization and preparation. You don't want anything or anyone to mess with your stage, so you probably need to be assertive when it comes to your preparation. Don't let your squad mates distract you. Don't let the Range Officer rush you. Get yourself in the zone.

Watch the shooters on the Super Squad. Usually, they draw and aim at a target, then load, and then move their hand to the gun a couple of times to practice, and so on. If you pay close attention, you will see these routines. This little mental ballet may seem silly but developing a routine can be a help. There is a strong correlation between this mental preparation and a good match performance.

The reason a routine is important is that it is another way for you to control your stress level. You get a final little check. Is your gun ready? Does your hand move to the holster smoothly? During your "make ready" routine you can make little adjustments and get comfortable with what you are about to do.

During your routine, do not allow yourself to be rushed or interrupted. Ignore all the chatter you may hear behind you. (Some squads can be rather rambunctious.) If you have active hearing protection, turn it off. You should eliminate those distractions and put your focus where it needs to be. Do not indicate that you are ready until you are actually ready. This is your time, and you need to use it effectively.

Before I indicate I am ready, I like to take a few deep breaths. I have heard from some medical professionals that having oxygenated blood is a good thing. I will take their word for it. People under stress sometimes take shallow breaths, and it is a good thing to counteract that tendency with some deep breaths before the stage gets started.

When the Range Officer gives you the "standby" command, you should think of that as your actual start signal. Your mind should be clear and waiting for the beep. The reason you should consider the "standby" command to be a start signal is that you should stop trying to do anything consciously at that point. You are ready to go when you get the beep. You never know when the beep will happen; you may get "short beeped" by a Range Officer. That is when they don't give you the required one second between the "standby" command and the actual start signal. If your mental start signal is the "standby" command, you can't get caught off guard by the beep. The stage has already started for you.

*It is important to be calm during the "make ready."*

# DEALING WITH
# MATCH PRESSURE

Everyone who has been to a USPSA match has felt the pressure. Match pressure is a real thing. It is an important thing. I suppose many people's natural inclination would be to say that match pressure doesn't affect them or that they aren't feeling pressure. This is rarely the case.

There are some very real chemical changes that take place in your body when you are standing at the line. This adrenaline rush, or whatever it is, can really mess you up. However, if you can learn to harness and have some control over match pressure, it can actually improve your performance. Let me briefly explain some of the effects of match pressure.

### Decision Making Is Difficult

Many people tend to "get stupid" under stress. In "real life," I suppose this can have tragic consequences. In a match scenario, it can have some extremely negative effects on your score (to put it really mildly). You can't possibly consciously think your way through all the little details of a stage while you are shooting it, even with no pressure bearing down on you. This is why there needs to be extensive training and programming before you shoot. When you add pressure into the scenario, decision making becomes even harder. I hope that you train well enough that there isn't anything you need to make a decision about as you are shooting.

## Your Hands Tremble

Adrenaline makes your hands shake. Normally, this will not have a very detrimental impact on accuracy. A two-handed hold will be relatively stable even if you have a little case of the shakes. However, one-handed accuracy can be seriously compromised by shaking. There isn't much you can do about this, you just need to hold that "wobble zone" right where you want to hit, and pull the trigger straight back.

## You Don't Have a Good Sense of Time

Match pressure will disrupt your sense of the passage of time. Slow can feel fast. Fast can feel slow. It is not uncommon for shooters to "feel slow," and then make the poor decision (see above) of trying to go faster to make up for it. The fact is, without a lot of experience, it is very difficult to tell if you are having a fast run or not when you are on the clock. It isn't uncommon for someone to entirely disregard marksmanship fundamentals (like aiming) because they "feel slow." I can't even count how many times I have had a guy in class acting that way. Of course, the best policy is just to shoot your own pace and let the time be what it is, but this is much more easily said than done.

## You Get Tense

Pressure makes people tense up. This tension then causes all sorts of other mistakes. It isn't difficult to see why this

is the case. If you put your holster on and practice drawing, try tensing your muscles up as much as you can, and
then practice drawing. You will likely have some problems. I most often see tension become an issue on close
range/high-speed shooting. When the shooting is going to
be fast, and you hear a bunch of other guys absolutely rail-
ing on a set of targets on a stage, you are probably going to
be tempted to match that pace. That can bring in the tension, and that can be accompanied by trigger freeze.

*I like to shake my hands out just before I indicate that
I am ready to shoot a stage. I feel like this helps release the
tension out of my whole body, not just my hands.*

## Physical Things Bother You a Lot Less
I have shot matches while sick, injured, tired, heat stroked,
etc. It is a miserable experience. However, when I step up
to the line and feel that pressure bearing down on me, that
physical discomfort goes away. Obviously, this is tempo-
rary. Just remember, if you are a little sore or a little tired,
you will not be nearly as tired or sore when you are actually shooting. Adrenaline will take care of that. If you are
injured, you should take care not to inflame the injury
while shooting a match. Adrenaline will maybe make you
Superman for one stage, but after that, whatever part of
your body you messed up is really going to hurt.

   You will also be physically stronger and faster when
hopped up on adrenaline. The effects of this can be good
or bad. You may be running fast enough that you overrun
a position if you aren't careful! You may try to gently press
the trigger straight back and find that you are punching the

s*** out of the trigger. I see this often, especially when a shooter misses a piece of steel. If they are feeling pressure, they will often start jerking the trigger worse than they were in the first place, because once they have that initial miss on steel the pressure level goes through the roof.

*I once saw a shooter (under stress) put a magazine into his Glock backward. The magazine didn't go into the gun on his first attempt to seat it, so he slapped the magazine as hard as he could. He realized what he was doing, but it was too late. He had hit the magazine into the gun so hard that he couldn't get it back out. It took a team of three people, 15 minutes to remove the magazine from the gun. Obviously, the shooter took a zero for the stage. Being extra strong due to adrenaline isn't always a positive thing.*

## Your Memory Can Be Affected

I should point out that an adrenaline dump can mess with your memory. I have seen guys under pressure only shoot one round at a target that requires two, or something goofy like that. After the stage, they will have no recollection that they did that. This is adrenaline, not someone being stupid (usually).

I think it is good to have as much of a memory of the stage as possible, because after shooting a match, you are probably going to want to take what you learned back to the training range. However, if you can't remember what you did on the stages, or how it felt to do that stuff, then you have less information to take to the training range. This is a good reason to video matches, so you can see exactly how you performed under pressure.

It should be clear, after reading the effects of pressure, that the negative things on the list can be very detrimental. The positive things are nice little bonuses, but they aren't strictly necessary for a good match. Clearly then, it is important to be able to manage the negative effects of pressure.

You should also understand that match pressure doesn't really come from the match, it comes from you. Shooters experience match pressure because they want to do well. Everyone is watching, after all, and you want to put up a good score.

It is a commonly held belief that the upper level shooters in the sport don't suffer from the effects of match pressure. This isn't true. The top shooters feel the effects of match pressure just as intensely as, and maybe more than, everyone else does. The reason is that the more time/money/energy you invest in the sport, the more pressure you will feel in a match situation. Certain things are expected of the higher level shooters. People want to see GMs tear up every stage. Even at a club match, when the local hotshot steps up to shoot, the squad quiets down to watch. Shooters notice this, even if only subconsciously. The higher you climb in the sport, the more match pressure you are going to feel.

## From Matthew Mink (IDPA National Champion, IPSC National Champion, IPSC World Shoot Gold Medalist)

### Going for it at ludicrous speed

*I have shot some stages over the years that can only be described as "ludicrous speed," to steal a quote from* Spaceballs. *I usually do it after I am mad at myself for screwing up some aspect of a stage previously. I tell someone, usually Ben, that I am going to own this stage with a vengeance. And 9 times out of 10, I do. I wish I could har-*  *ness that on every stage. I believe it is a function of mindset, where I not only execute everything near the limit of human function, but completely believe I can do it.*

There are a few strategies for managing this match pressure. The most popular strategy in USPSA is the common advice to "shoot your own game." Using this strategy, you effectively train yourself to ignore the things happening around you. You don't listen to other shooters' times or track the scores. You tune all that stuff out and just shoot each stage the best you can. I think that, generally speaking, you should go to a match and follow this advice. Shoot your own game. I should warn you though; eventually you will be put in a competitive situation where you simply can't ignore your surroundings. It may be that you get good at the club level, and then you go to your first major match. It is tough to pretend that it isn't a major match. If you find yourself in this situation, the pressure can magnify. You have avoided pressure for so long that it may be more difficult to actually deal with it when you go to a big match.

A book by Lanny Bassam is popular in USPSA circles. It outlines a system for improving your "mental management." Much of Lanny's work focuses on improving your "self-image" as a competitor. This book has been floating around for years, and some shooters think it is absolutely the key to victory. Other shooters like the book *The Inner Game of Tennis*. In any event, there are books out there devoted to mental management, and some people think that they help you a great deal. I haven't gotten much out of them myself, but others have.

## From Keith Garcia (USPSA Grand Master)

### *Shoot the Sights!*

*Wandering through the SHOT show the day after winning $50,000 at the 3 Gun Nation "Rumble on the Range," I kept hearing the same question over and over; Do you get nervous before you shoot? Truthfully, I do not. I used to feel stress, and I think it is perfectly normal when you start competing. The key to mastering the mental game and getting past the nerves is practice, and lots of it. By dry-firing, live-firing, and visualization, you can overcome the nerves. You need to push yourself in practice to the point where your shooting breaks down. Once you know that point, slow down 2 to 5 percent. Practice*

*at that level, own it; understand what the trigger feels like and the sights look like at that speed. Once you have that imprinted in your subconscious, you can relax and simply "shoot the sights." Let the other shooters try to become heroes while you shoot strong and consistent.*

The best method I have found for learning to shoot under pressure is to practice shooting under pressure. This may seem to be so self-evident that it is ridiculous to mention, but if you think about the advice I gave, it may not be obvious how to carry through with it. It is very common for shooters to get comfortable shooting at the club level, and then no longer feel much pressure at those matches. Those same shooters then go to majors and melt under the pressure they bring with them. So how are they supposed to practice for that? Many people might think the only way to practice operating under that sort of pressure is to just keep going to major matches. I suppose that is one solution, but it could take years to learn how to handle the pressure under those circumstances.

What I like to do instead is to convince myself that the first drill I go shoot, when practicing, is the one that counts. My first run of the day is how good I am. There are no mulligans, no do-overs, and no warm-ups. I just go out and shoot the first run of the day just as if it is the first run at Nationals. If you can get yourself into that mindset and really internalize it, you will bring the same pressure with you to the practice range. Then, instead of taking years to learn to operate under pressure, you can shorten that learning curve to a few months. This is the best method I have personally found, and it works well for those people I know that have tried it.

It happened to me! The first time I found myself in the lead at USPSA Nationals, the pressure was unbelievable. I was up to shoot a 12-round stage. It was one of those six shots, reload, six shots, strong hand only stages. One of the targets was at 20 yards. It was my plan to reload, and then go straight to the 20-yard target for the strong hand only portion of the stage. I was sweating and shaking. I am not a wuss or anything; it was just that the adrenaline had taken over. After getting the "make ready" command, I held my gun up strong hand only and took a sight picture on the 20-yard target. The sight was shaking so much (because my hand was shaking) that it wouldn't even stay on the target. I stood there, just like that, breathing slowly, until I was able to get my body under control. I reminded myself that the best strategy would be to just let the front sight wobble around and squeeze the trigger right through it. There was nothing else I could do about it. I executed the stage just the way I planned. When I got to the long target on the strong hand only part of the stage, I saw the sight wobbling, but just squeezed through it as I had planned. It turned out I won the stage doing that.

For the guys chasing a national championship, the hardest thing to do is to win the first one. As soon as you get that monkey off your back, things get a lot easier. This is why the same people tend to win over and over again. The great Rob Leatham has won more national titles than I have fingers and toes to count them on. He did that because of his skill level, but he also has another important advantage. He sees himself as a champion because he wins all the time. It is a cycle of winning. Once you can break into that cycle, it is tough for other people to break you out of it.

Many of the techniques I advocate are effective because of match pressure. I have seen shooters make some serious mistakes due to the pressure. That "scoop draw" that you can do every time like clockwork on your home range turns into a DQ waiting to happen when you are under pressure. Match pressure is the reason you need to visualize a stage over and over and over again. Simply knowing where to go and what targets to shoot isn't good enough. Your subconscious needs to be programmed to shoot the stage for you.

Ideally, if you train yourself to shoot through the match pressure, you will be able to step to the line and simply do what you know how to do. You can't ask for more than that.

If I had to sum up mental management in to one word, I think it would be "discipline." Learn to be a disciplined shooter, and do what you are supposed to do absolutely, no matter what. No matter what the stakes in the match, you always execute your techniques to the best possible effect. This comes from diligently training yourself, always with discipline in mind.

So often I have shooters ask me about the "mental game," like it is an entirely separate thing that you will work on by itself. I suppose you could do it that way. You could sit by yourself, close your eyes, and rehearse your shooting to make sure you don't mess stuff up on game day. You can sit in the hotel room the night before a big match and mentally rehearse each stage. You can visualize perfect runs on every single stage in the match.

I think the best way to think about "the mental game," is to conceptualize it as this thing that is always happening. It is always operating. Every time you practice your shooting, or think about shooting, you are working on your mental game whether you know it or not. You should spend that time perfecting your technical skill and mentally preparing yourself to execute that skill under pressure. You shouldn't spend too much time worrying about how fast some other guy is at this or that thing. You should focus on doing your best every single run. By building up your skills and confidence, you should be good enough that you have a good performance on the big day.

## From Blake Miguez (USPSA National Champion and IPSC World Champion)

### *Remember to Have Fun!*

*Blake Miguez having fun!*

*Unlike many of the pro shooters out on the circuit, shooting is not my whole life. I have lots of things outside of shooting that I really enjoy. I try not to take any of this too seriously and just want to have fun. Don't get me wrong, I love going fast, and I love winning. I enjoy my rivalry with some other shooters. I feed off it. But at the end of the day, I shoot for fun.*

# MANAGING
# YOURSELF DURING
# A MAJOR MATCH

For many USPSA shooters, the road doesn't end with shooting club matches. I hope the people reading this move on and shoot state or regional matches. Hell, shoot Nationals if you can. If you have the opportunity, then going to international matches run under IPSC rules is great fun and a worthwhile experience. Obviously, the major match environment is very different from the local level. There are dedicated Range Officers working the match. There is usually a chronograph station to make sure your ammunition is legal. There are more stages than a club match. Most importantly, everyone takes it more seriously. It is common for people to shoot well at the local level, and then melt under the pressure of a major match.

If you want to go to lots of big matches, then that is going to require travel. Depending on the distances involved, that usually means long car rides if you live in the middle of the country. Shooters commonly drive 10 or more hours to matches. Personally, I usually fly if it is more than about a 12-hour drive, but not always. I think the key issue is dealing with all the gear that you need to bring along. Driving makes it easy to bring a backup gun (a good idea) and plenty of ammo. You can bring gun cleaning stuff. You can bring a cooler. You can bring a chair. When you drive, you are usually going to get to bring more stuff than when you fly.

Flying domestically in the United States for USPSA matches isn't as challenging as you might think if you have never flown with a gun. You just need to declare the gun, pack it per FAA regulations, and you should be good to go. The airlines try to limit ammunition to 11 pounds per person, but in my experience, they don't work that hard to enforce the regulation. In any event, you can ship match ammunition to the match location, and as long as the Match Director is cool, they will receive your ammo for you, so you can attend the match.

The problem with flying is the limitation on the gear you can bring. Unless you don't care about bag fees for checking multiple bags, you are going to have to make some choices about what goes. I think at minimum you should bring a gun, backup gun, belt, magazines, a cleaning kit, safety equipment, and ammo. You pick up whatever else you might need when you are on location.

Another challenge to contend with at major matches (aside from the shooting related things) is the weather. Most major matches take place during the summer months. Things can be extremely unpleasant, especially as you go farther south. Triple digit heat, high humidity, and thunderstorms are all possibilities. You may need to be out in the elements for ten or twelve hours straight. You don't need to just be outside during this time, you need to have your head in the game. It is hard to be at 100 percent the whole time, but there are some things you can do.

Obviously, you need to be ready for the weather. A well-prepared shooter should have things in their range bag to help them. It is a good idea to have a poncho in your bag. One of the three-dollar cheapo ponchos is fine. Just buy one, stick it in your range bag, and forget about it. It will be there six months down the line when you need it.

Bring plenty of food and water to the range. I am not a nutritionist, but I think most of them would tell you to eat a little bit at a time, frequently throughout the day. I like to bring granola, fruit, trail mix, and those sorts of things along with me to the match. I also bring plenty of fluid. I keep drinking the whole day. If you get a little bit hungry, then you should eat a little bit. Eating a lot of food is usually a bad idea. For that reason, I almost always skip lunch at major matches. Many matches have big barbeque lunches available. It may be tempting, but filling up on heavy food during the match can be detrimental. You want your body ready to rock and roll, not busy digesting a big meal.

Remember, you need to keep your energy up the entire day. It isn't enough just to be there; you need to be all there. You need to have a clear head, and that will not happen if you are dehydrated. Keep drinking water. You should constantly be peeing.

Make sure you show up early to the major match. You want ample time to go look at stages and get a sense of the whole setup. If there are complicated moving targets, it is best to see them in operation. That means that you need to get there a day early and see other people shooting at them, because you won't be allowed to activate them during your walkthrough.

During the match, remember that everyone will be shooting under the same conditions. If you have a bad stage or make a mistake, then brush it off and continue on with the match. I have yet to see anyone have a perfect match, so don't think that you need to be perfect in order to do well.

# SHOOTING AN "OPEN" GUN

"O pen" guns (the "race" guns with red dot sights and compensators) are fundamentally no different from Production guns. In terms of technique, there are a few little differences. This section isn't designed to totally prepare someone to shoot Open. This is just a way to explain how some of the techniques already mentioned would be applied to an Open gun platform.

*Jay Hirshberg with his Open gun.*

First, dot sights make things simpler in terms of aiming. The list of aiming options that I proposed earlier on in the book is much shorter when it comes to dot guns. Most targets are dealt with using a target focus and simply putting the dot where you want the bullet to hit. There is no point in changing optical focus around between the dot itself and the target. Dot sights are designed so that the shooter can focus on the target the entire time. This fact alone is a substantial reason that dot sights are so much faster, especially as the distance to the target increases.

On the other hand, dot sights are generally regarded as a good learning tool. The dot will show you even the tiniest movement when the trigger is pressed. The dot will show you exactly how much the gun is bouncing around as you move into a position. It is astonishing how much and how clearly you can see this when you utilize a dot sight.

Some people have an issue with shooting target focused all the time. It is a natural tendency to want to pull your focus back toward the dot. This isn't productive for shooting Open, and can be a bit of a time waster. One way to counteract that potential problem is to cover the front of the scope with a bit of cardboard. You should be able to shoot normally, provided you focus on the target and shoot with both eyes open. If you inadvertently move your focus back to the dot, it will be really obvious, and you will be able to make a correction.

Next, Open guns are loud. When I say loud, I mean extremely loud. This isn't a big consideration in and of itself, but it is a potential consideration, especially for newer shooters. A shooter that is still trying to overcome sensitivity to the blast and noise of a gun may have a hard time dealing with an Open gun. "Double plugging" (wearing two sets of hearing protection) is one possible solution for this problem. It is important to be aware that the added noise of Open guns can have an effect on some shooters.

## From Taran Butler (USPSA Grand Master, multiple time 3-gun National Champion)

*Shooting Open and Production is about as far apart as you can get in the USPSA divisions. The mindset in shooting Open has more emphasis on speed. Having the dot, up to thirty-one rounds in the gun before a reload, and the low recoil because of the compensator makes a shooter want to push a little harder because it's more forgiving on the penalties and much easier for the tight shots and steel targets. On the other hand, in Production you probably put yourself at ninety percent of your speed, and keep the emphasis much more on trying to hit "A"s and trying not to get ahead of the sights. You hardly have any extra rounds for pick-up shots on steel because you're limited to a third as many rounds as the Open gun. Regardless of either division, the ones that win have the mindset to be smooth and accurate.*

Finally, malfunction clearance with an Open gun is a little bit different. If your specific gun is equipped with a

"slide racker," then obviously that is the best way to manipulate the slide. There isn't any reason not to use it. Another added benefit of the slide racker is that it helps "prop" the pistol for a table start. The scope mount, on the other hand, can make things a little more difficult. Scope mounts can obstruct your view into the chamber of the pistol. When you are trying to diagnose an issue with the gun, it is a problem not to be able to see. You might need to slightly rotate the gun in your hand so you can get a little bit better view of what is going on in the chamber.

The slide racker isn't the only ergonomic advantage an Open gun has. Magwells, custom grips, and thumb rests can all help you get the gun set up to fit you really well. Sure, you can modify Production guns to some extent. This is nothing like what you can and should do to an Open gun.

# EQUIPMENT ISSUES

Equipment isn't the focus of this book, but people always have equipment questions. I want to do my absolute best to answer them.

## Selecting a Gun

The first equipment question that people tend to wonder about is how to pick a gun. If you don't already have a gun that you think is suitable for USPSA, then you will want to get one straight away. That way you don't waste time being frustrated with gear that doesn't work properly.

I think the first decision you are going to need to make is which division you like the idea of the most. If you want to shoot a custom "race gun" in Limited or Open Division, you have a different menu of options than you would have in Production Division.

I think the easiest thing to do is figure out what the winners in your division use, and either copy that gear, or figure out why that gear doesn't work for you. For example, in Open Division your default choice should be a custom 2011. No, you don't need to shoot that. It's true that you could customize some other gun and make it work for the division, but without good reason to do so, I really don't see the point.

In Production Division, you probably have the most options. There are high-level shooters using guns from a relatively large number of manufacturers. Obviously, someone could be competitive with any one of these guns, but I think you should pick the gun that is best for you.

The first big choice to make for Production is whether you want a striker fired plastic gun or a DA/SA metal gun. The striker fired guns are generally simple to manipulate and simple to learn with only one trigger mode. Most people find the DA/SA guns to be easy to shoot accurately, especially in SA mode. Deciding between these two schools isn't something that anyone can do for you. You need to play around with a few different guns, and pick the gun you like the best. Shooters at your local club will have a few different options, and I can't imagine they wouldn't show you their gun.

For striker fired pistols, the dominant choice is going to be a Glock. There are quite a few options in terms of customization and plenty of aftermarket support. If you go the DA/SA route, you are likely going to end up with a CZ/Tanfoglio. The CZ pattern guns have the most support and the most options available.

This leaves out the Sig 226, Sig 320, Beretta 92 (my old gun of choice), M&P, Bersa, Grandpower, XD, HK, and tons of others. There are so many viable choices, yet few popular ones!

If you are attracted to a gun that isn't a Glock or CZ/Tanfoglio, then I only have one bit of advice. Before you go down the road of learning on a gun that isn't a dominant choice, plan out the purchase to the last detail. You will need a good holster, spare magazines, spare parts, sights, perhaps extended controls, and so forth. If you can't get all the stuff you need for your gun, then pick something else.

When I was shooting a Beretta, I used extended magazine basepads, fiber front sights, extended magazine releases, and DOH holsters. If I hadn't been able to get all of that equipment, then it would have been a deal breaker for me. I would have gone a different direction with the gun I was shooting. Those additional options made a gun that was otherwise unsuitable, ready for competition.

*Examples of Production guns.*

In any event, if you are thinking about buying a gun, the most important element is how that gun fits your hand. You can change the sights. You can work on the trigger. The toughest thing to modify is going to be the frame. Sure, with some guns you can change the backstrap out, extend the magazine release, or even get a wider/narrower grip panel. That is all a possibility. However, you should select your gun primarily based on how it fits your hand and whether it lets you effectively grip it. I see too many shooters with huge hands shooting a thin gripped CZ. It doesn't make sense to do that if you can't grip the f***ing gun properly. Please pick a gun that you can actually grip effectively because that is the hardest thing to change.

Check to make sure you can reach the trigger. Make sure you can reach the controls. Make sure the safety doesn't eat your hand alive when you shoot the gun.

### Sights . . . Fiber or Not?

I think a common question from shooters is regarding whether they should have fiber optic sights or not.

I personally prefer to use fiber, and I recommend it. It gives you a few more options in terms of how to aim your gun. Using the fiber to rail on close range targets is simple and easy. I wouldn't like not having that option.

However, if you find it difficult to get a front sight focus on your fiber sight, then you might want to stick with iron sights, at least until you get the issue sorted out. If you aren't in control of your focal changes, then you are going to have quite a hard time shooting long shots. I think this is the most common failing I see regarding fiber sights.

I should also point out that the gigantic fiber bulbs that some shooters use are probably not the best for USPSA. You don't need a gigantic bulb in order to aim with a fiber sight. You just need an easy aiming reference for doing close range blasting.

### Modifying Your Gun

I already touched on it briefly, but you shouldn't hesitate to modify your gun to some degree if the gun requires it.

First and foremost, you need to be able to reach the controls with the notable exception of the slide stop. You don't strictly need to be able to reach the slide stop with your strong hand thumb for USPSA competition. It may even be nice to have the slide stop out of reach entirely, so you aren't inadvertently pushing on it and inducing malfunctions.

The sights and trigger are other things you may want to change. Most USPSA shooters use fiber front and flat black rear sights. I use adjustable rear sights on my current guns and like them just fine. If you like having that feature, then it might be worth the effort to install sights.

Modifying the trigger is something that you probably will want to do. Having an excessively heavy trigger isn't a bad thing early on in your shooting career. It can help you learn trigger control. You will want to move away from that as you get better.

Obviously, if you modify your trigger, take care not to damage the gun or render the gun unreliable. The best advice I can give, aside from that, is to focus on other things rather than the trigger pull weight. Sure, it is nice to have a trigger that is easier to press. That makes it easier to press straight, as well. However, you probably shouldn't go so far as to bend trigger return springs or polish the internals right up to the point where the gun is borderline unreliable. Having a trigger return that pushes back into your finger can give you some feedback on what the trigger is doing. Polishing things until they are a few thousand rounds away from wearing out will just cause you to need to do the work over again.

Finally, I don't like it when a gun is restricted only to very soft (Federal) primers. You may need to borrow ammo in a pinch. You may run out of soft primers. Anything could happen. It isn't worth a marginally lighter trigger to compromise your gun in that way.

## Ammunition

Ammunition is something that shooters will never stop tinkering with, despite the fact it doesn't offer much of an advantage.

If you are serious about shooting a lot, you are almost certainly going to need to reload your ammunition, just so you have a viable way of training. I personally shoot coated bullets, over cheap powder, over whatever primer I can find, loaded into too many times fired range brass. This is pretty much the cheapest solution. I have used the same load for a few years and it works fine. I then buy ammunition for matches, so I know I am getting quality stuff.

If shooters commit one sin with reloads, it is that they constantly are messing around with it. Find a load you can afford and that you like for whatever reason, and then make a bunch of it. There is no need to be constantly making adjustments. Every time you use a new load, you should test it to make sure it is accurate, reliable, and chronographs properly. This is quite a bit of energy to spend during your limited training time. If you don't mess with a load, you don't need to change anything.

I think many shooters make the mistake of scraping the power floor for whatever division they are in. I don't think you want to do that. You should shoot ammunition that easily makes the power factor requirements, so you aren't worried about the chronograph. I used to play the game of shooting the softest possible load, but to be honest it wasn't worth the headaches. If you shoot ammo that is a bit hotter than it needs to be, you will be perfectly comfortable with it on match day.

## Selecting and Setting Up Belt/Holster/Pouches

You should select your belt, holster, and magazine pouches with every bit as much care as you select your gun. You want the support gear you use to keep your equipment in a stable position and retain that gear while you run. You will also need to be able to quickly draw magazines and your gun out of this gear.

For the belt, people almost universally use the CR Speed or DAA double belt systems. They come with a Velcro inner belt, and then a more rigid outer belt. I strongly recommend a belt like this. It will keep all of your gear in a consistent place regardless of where your belt loops are on your pants that day.

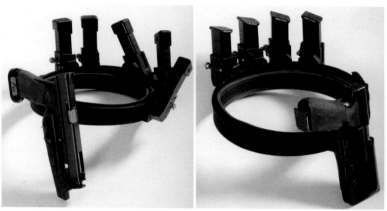

*A couple examples of commonly used gear.*

For a holster, I like a dropped and offset system with some adjustability. You should be able to adjust the gun position enough that you can get a comfortable position for the gun. The holster should then be trusted to keep that adjustment indefinitely.

Finally, you have a plethora of viable options for magazine pouches. Ghost, CR Speed, DAA, and a few other companies all carry magazine pouches for USPSA competition. I have seen workable setups with any brand of pouch. Each brand and pouch style has advantages and disadvantages. If you are shooting a low capacity division, you should probably stay away from the heavier metal pouches.

Ideally, you get your gear set up so it gets out of your way. Equipment should be positioned to where your hands naturally want to go when you do quick gun handling. If it doesn't feel right, then fix it until it does. Don't be afraid to modify pouches. They are relatively cheap and easy to replace.

## Your Stuff Needs to Work

The fact is many shooters show up at matches with gear they know doesn't work. Simply put, it is a stupid thing to do. Don't be that guy. Everyone's stuff has issues occasionally. If you are serious about shooting, you are going to put lots of wear and tear on your guns and support equipment. Over time, as things wear out, gear that was impeccable won't be so great any longer. As issues crop up, you should fix them. What is unacceptable is to not address problems as they arise.

If you are serious about major matches, get a second set of equipment. If you have a gun that you like and that works well, buy another one and set it up just the same. That way you'll have a backup gun if something goes wrong with your primary. You may even consider using one set of gear just for practice. That way all the real wear and tear goes onto the practice setup. You can learn what parts wear out and what things to look for on that specific type of gun.

If you have a malfunction, you shouldn't ignore it. Try your best to figure out what happened, so you don't have the same problem come up on match day. If a part needs replacing, fix it.

## Modification to Your Gun

It is important to know that many manufacturers offer different parts. You might want a bigger safety or a smaller mag button or whatever. If it works within the rules of the game you are playing, then make your gun fit you better.

*Magwell, fiber optic, stippling, oversized mag release.*

Don't be afraid to modify your gear. Be sure you don't compromise the reliability of your gear when you modify it. However, within that constraint, do what you can. Many people find it difficult to take a hacksaw or a grinder to expensive gear they bought. Don't worry about it. If your mag pouches have too much material on them, cut some off. If you don't like white dots on your sights, take a Sharpie to them. Your gear is a tool, nothing more.

Another caution regarding equipment is that you need to know what you are doing to modify it. If you don't know how to do a trigger job on your 1911, send it to someone who does. You don't want to end up with a fully automatic pistol when you were just trying to get the trigger lighter. There are resources available online all over the place to help you learn to modify your equipment. Consult them carefully before you undertake any modification.

One very common equipment problem I see is people that have pouches and holsters adjusted so that it is very difficult to get the gun and mags out. The proper tension settings should allow you to easily get the gun out of the holster but keep the gun securely in the holster when you don't want to take it out. Don't settle for anything less than perfect adjustment.

### Fiber or Not?

One equipment discussion that never seems to end is about what sights to put on your pistol. The majority of shooters seem to have some sort of fiber optic. If you take a second to look over the different aiming options listed in the "Target Transitions" section, you can see why this is. Fiber optic sights give you more options. Personally, I use and recommend fiber. However, I don't like the really huge fiber rods or having a bright fiber optic sight. The brighter the fiber, the more it seems to "wash out" the front sight post. This is especially true in bright sunlight. What I like to do is to dull the top of the fiber rod with a Sharpie. This makes the fiber appear a bit duller in bright sunlight and keeps it from "popping off" the front sight post. If you find yourself unable to get a hard front sight focus at speed while using fiber, then I recommend you dump the fiber and go with flat black sights instead.

## DA/SA Triggers

There seems to be quite a bit of discussion about double action trigger systems like Sigs or CZs. These triggers are very workable, but you may end up needing to use a different technique for each trigger mode. If you are a "trigger slapper" in the single action mode, you may need to adopt a different technique for the double action mode. In any event, it can help you a lot to treat each mode separately.

# ODDS AND ENDS

The more astute readers will notice there have been a few topics omitted.

The standard marksmanship chart to diagnose errors that many people rely on to aid in learning marksmanship was not in this book. Not until now anyway. If you don't know what chart I am talking about, it is right here.

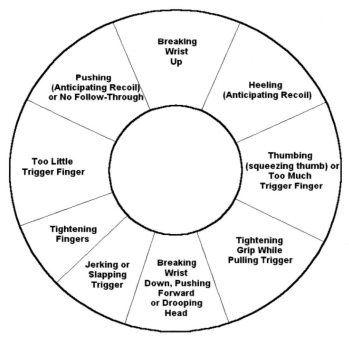

*Source: US Army Marksmanship Unit Training Guide tutorial.*
*This material is in the public domain.*

This chart isn't really all that helpful for a USPSA shooter. As soon as you go beyond standing static on a firing line doing slow fire on a single target, this chart doesn't really help a whole lot. For example, when shooting quickly at a tough target, you may miss over the top of the target. This chart would indicate that "breaking wrist up" is the problem, but my experience in USPSA would tell me that usually it is a matter of not letting the sights settle out of recoil for the second shot. People get on the trigger too early when transitioning onto a target, they aim in the wrong spots, they have the gun bouncing up and down when they move, and so on. There are so many different technique problems that interact in different ways, depending on the scenario, that it is very tough to come up with a chart for USPSA shooters.

I can't count how many times I have had a guy in a class hit a left delta on a target and immediately think that it is trigger control. No matter that the target was five yards away and the guy can shoot a softball sized group as fast as he can pull the trigger at that distance. The chart leads to people guessing about what is causing a problem instead of actually learning what is causing problems.

The best way to learn to diagnose your own shooting is to learn to "call your shots." If you quit blinking and start looking for the sights in recoil, you are going to see many interesting things happening. If you have a gut feeling that you saw your sights do something funky, but you can't recall the specifics, then you need to trust your gut. A lot of learning can be done at almost an instinctual level.

Another issue that was ignored is that of "breathing." Many marksmanship manuals, or references like that, will list breathing as a fundamental of target shooting.

For practical shooting purposes, breathing isn't an issue that we want to worry about in regards to marksmanship. The effect of breathing on marksmanship fundamentals is so marginal that it doesn't warrant attention for our purposes. Not to mention, it is difficult to control your breathing on a stage where you have to sprint a few yards, then shoot, then sprint, then shoot, etc. What is important is that you keep breathing. This may sound self-evident, but it isn't. Many times, guys will hold their breath on stages while they wait for the start signal. After a few seconds of holding your breath, you are putting yourself at a disadvantage when you start the stage. Take care to keep breathing.

There is another issue that is mentioned quite a bit in various marksmanship manuals, and that is "follow through." Follow through has been ignored in this book. I am not entirely certain what it is. It is defined in many different ways depending on whom you ask:

1. Calling the shot.
2. Getting a second sight picture after shooting a shot.
3. Getting a second sight picture and prepping the trigger for the next shot.
4. Keeping the gun up and on target after shooting.
5. Holding the gun still while the shot breaks.

(This is not an inclusive list.)

There is no agreed-upon definition. There isn't even a definition that I would say is prevalent. I can't recall ever having a conversation with a shooter or student where they mentioned "follow through," without me asking exactly what it was that they mean by that word. I don't know what people mean when they use it. I don't use it myself because nobody would know what I mean. I don't see any use for the term. That's why it wasn't included in any of the preceding material.

Another thing that many may feel is missing from this book is when to "slow down" or" speed up" your shooting. Ideas about when to slow down and speed up can be misinterpreted very easily, and for that reason, they were generally avoided. It is true; sometimes a shooter is just shooting too quickly to be effective. Spraying bullets around without any aiming reference isn't a good idea. At least slow yourself down to the speed of some effective aiming tool. The reverse can also be true. Shooting a stage in 60 seconds, that the top guys are shooting in 12 seconds, is just plain too slow. Go faster! The important thing for you to understand is why someone is going too fast or too slow, and what aiming method they need to use to get the hits the most efficiently.

Yet another issue that some may feel is missing is any discussion of "Point Shooting." The same problem that occurred with "follow through" occurs with point shooting. It is difficult to even pin down a definition of what "point shooting" is. Some people say it is aiming without a visual reference at all. Others say it is looking through the sights at the target. It is difficult to discuss "point shooting," and pointless to try to disentangle that term from all the different connotations it already has. If you read the section on how to aim at targets during the discussion of target transitions, you will find plenty of ideas in there that certainly fit within someone's definition of point shooting. I have avoided attaching that term to it because that will generate confusion.

I didn't talk at all about handgun ballistics. At longer ranges, handgun ballistics can have a dramatic effect on point of aim/point of impact considerations. These issues fall outside the scope of this book. It is important to have at least a rudimentary understanding of ballistics to be an extremely successful handgun shooter, but for the fundamental applications, it isn't a huge deal. It is only important that you know where your gun hits, in relation to the sights, at every distance you shoot at.

Finally, there are a myriad of issues surrounding someone's eyes. Some people have glasses, contacts, LASIK, 20/20 vision, or any number of situations. Many people are cross dominant (their dominant eye is opposite their dominant hand). People commonly ask about shooting with one eye open versus both open. There are enough issues surrounding your eyes to take up an entire book. Generally speaking, these issues are best left to the individual to sort out on their own with a couple of exceptions. The overwhelming weight of opinion in practical shooting sports is that it is best to shoot with both eyes open. Your field of vision will be wider, and this (in theory), aids in your target transition speed. On the other hand, it is workable to shoot with only one eye open. Not everyone can shoot with both eyes open because they find it difficult to focus on the front sight blade. If you are unable to shoot with both eyes open, one eye open will have to suffice.

### One eye only?

*It is common for shooters to use both eyes open normally, and then close an eye to aid in aiming when shooting a difficult shot. This technique requires practice, just like any other, as you may close, and then open an eye a few times over the course of a stage. It may be easier just to keep an eye shut for the entire stage, if you plan to close that eye at any point during that stage. Experiment and see what works for you.*

*"Magic Dot" on lens of shooting glasses.*

## From Lori Casper (USPSA & IDPA Master)

*I found that when I first started shooting pistols, I had trouble keeping both eyes open. Shutting one eye helped with the "ghost" image of my pistol but doing so for an entire match caused strain in my face muscles and loss of peripheral vision on the side with the closed eye. I found it very helpful to use a product such as Magic Dot, which is a small round translucent plastic that adheres to the inside of your shooting glasses. When applied over the appropriate eye, it subtly screens it out of the aiming process while maintaining the key advantages of two-eyed vision, depth perception, and peripheral vision. It also eliminates the face muscle strain. Many have found using semi-transparent style tape works equally well.*

# PRE-IGNITION PUSH CORRECTION

This entire chapter was initially sent to me by Chris Bartolo. This was printed in the first edition of *Practical Pistol*. I still think it has value, so it appears again here.

*Chris "G-Man" Bartolo.*

Anyway, I was getting some feedback from him on an early version of this book, and he had some great ideas. He had already written this document and used it to try to help out some other shooters. I felt this information needed to be made available to shooters, so I have included it here.

**From Chris Bartolo (USPSA Grand Master).**

*First off, I'll say that different things are going to work for different people, so what I suggest may or may not help, but it's worth exploring. I can say that some variation or combination of these has always worked when I've had someone who really wanted to get better.*

Whenever possible, if I'm helping someone with a pre-ignition push, I like to have them shoot a .22 Long Rifle. I normally work with folks who are already at the range and may have just shot poorly on a qualification course. In other words, they're warmed up and doing whatever it is that's causing the problem by the time we talk. If I'm going to work with someone at the start of the day, I'll let them shoot a bit to show me the problem. At that point, I'll hand them a .22 and have them shoot with zero pressure. Normally, the very first shot will be a pre-ignition push that's really obvious, and they'll say something like, "Oh, that's what I'm doing wrong." Essentially, that's the first time they've ever called a shot. It didn't go where they wanted it to, but at least they know where it went. They may have been "flinching" for years and simply didn't know what it looked like. After that I'll let them shoot a couple of magazines (still with the .22) to get comfortable, and maybe have them shoot a freestyle group or two from 25 yards. Then they see it's actually easy to keep all their hits inside something the size of our "A" zone if you don't have bad habits. At that point, I'll have them go back to their normal gun, and start with slower, controlled shots, and have them work up in speed. Normally, within a mag or two, they'll throw one low and left and they'll look at me and say "I knew it." That awareness is the key to fixing the problem; you've got to see it, to fix it. At the very least, at this point, they're aware of the problem and know it when it happens.

As something of an aside, if they didn't see it when they had the pre-ignition push, it means they're blinking. That's a different problem. The short answer is to double plug/muff. Stick with the .22, and have them think about the corners of their eyes while shooting the gun in the general vicinity of the target. Steel or another reactive target (clay birds, etc.) seems to help some folks with this as they want to see the hit, so they're less likely to blink. Indoors and loud guns (hey Open shooters!) make this worse.

Now they know what it looks like when things go wrong, and it's time to work on making things go right. They do this by learning to consistently call shots. I'll have folks shoot at nothing but the backstop and have them track the front sight, i.e., don't tell me where the shot went, tell me what the front sight did. I then like for them to shoot deliberate shots with the sights intentionally misaligned. Put a target at something like 15 to 20 yards and have them make the sight picture so the front sight appears to be nearly touching either side of the notch in the rear sight. Do the same with the front sight well above the top and well below the top of the rear sight . . . enough that you can see it's high or low from the side. They're usually pretty shocked that they get hits near the center of the target with the sights poorly aligned. Then I'll have them shoot deliberate shots (start the trigger press and never stop until it breaks) while moving their hands in a circle (seems to usually be more of an oval). Imagine tracing a circle five inches in diameter around the "A" zone with your front sight. Keep the hands moving as the shot breaks. Again, people are surprised how close to the center the hits are.

All of this teaches the brain that if you have a decent trigger press, and even reasonably well-aligned sights on the target, you're going to get solid hits (for USPSA/IDPA type targets and distances). If you can hit the "A" zone while making a five-inch circle with the gun, you can certainly hit it if the gun is moving a tiny fraction of an inch in your wobble zone while holding it freestyle!

Now our shooter's brain knows that the sights don't have to be "perfect" to get a good hit up to a certain point. This is why a good shooter can rip off crazy fast splits on close targets. They learn that at something like three to five yards, you only very generally need to see the sights aligned to get good hits. Just a flash that everything is in sort of the right place, and your brain will press the trigger for you. You will gradually learn how much you can and cannot accept and still make the shot required at the moment.

*Chris "G-Man" Bartolo.*

I talk about this last part, because the vast majority of people I see struggling with this problem are stopping their trigger press to get the sights lined up "just right." Then they are accelerating/mashing through the trigger when things look perfect (snatching the shot). Once you stop the trigger press, you are starting from zero. It's similar to simply smashing the trigger from the fully forward/reset position . . . not quite as bad, but close to it. If your brain knows that the sight picture is acceptable, you can simply press smoothly and let the hits happen, even though visually the sights appear to be moving around a lot on the target.

To help with that last one, I'll sometimes have people shoot with a target backward (so they can't see the scoring zones). I tell them, "Just hit the cardboard anywhere." Since they're not so focused on that one little spot in the center, or on getting the sights perfectly aligned with it, they'll shoot a nice group. When we teach low light, we often get folks that shoot a fist-sized knot on their target, and they can barely see the target . . . there's a lesson in that!

One thing that I've started doing more recently is to use a large steel target in place of the backward cardboard target. If I can, I'll actually set the range so that I have several pieces of steel in several sizes so that I can trick my shooter. I'll start them on the big piece and get them making good hits, then transition to a smaller piece . . . then an even smaller piece. Before they know it, I have them consistently hitting something like a six- to eight-inch steel plate at 25 yards. When I point this out, they're usually shocked to realize what they're actually capable of. They laugh when I point out how I tricked them.

There is one demonstration that I do which doesn't require a gun, and it proves that everyone is a "flincher." I learned it from a guy in San Antonio who happened to have an Olympic Gold Medal for pistol shooting on his mantle. I may have to get someone to volunteer so we can video it and post it online. Basically, it involves me pushing on someone's outstretched palm. I tell them I'm going to gently bump their hand, and I do that a few times until they get used to it. Then, while still talking, I miss their hand, and they about fall on their face. The next time, I tell them which time I'm going to miss, and they still flinch a little. That's what we're dealing with when we shoot. Your body knows it's going to get a push, and it wants to stay in balance, so it's going to push back. You just have to make that happen after ignition, and things will be great.

# FURTHER
# DEVELOPMENT

It is my sincere hope that you get a lot out of this book. The concepts covered may seem complicated, and I suppose some of them are. The important thing is that you are able to internalize these things, and then work on them. The journey to the very top of the ranks in competitive shooting will take years, and the complexity of the issues involved is the reason it takes so long.

It is important that you study each of the issues discussed in this book in isolation. Work hard on your stage breakdown. Work hard on your programming. Learn to shoot on-the-move. If you have questions about a technique, flip back to the relevant section and try to figure it out.

What really makes the difference is being able to do all of the techniques without having to think about it. It all needs to come together at some point, so keep working toward that goal. You need to understand how all the individual technique sections of this book intertwine. How does grip affect trigger control? What does stage programming have to do with draw technique?

As you develop, diagnosing problems is important. If you don't understand the problem that you are having, you can't possibly fix it. There are books and forums out there

that are full of drills for you to try. Going out and bang-
ing off fifty thousand rounds a year on drills is one thing.
However, understanding technique will allow you to come
up with your own drills. It will allow you to drive your
own improvement. You need to think about this stuff. You
need to understand this stuff. The more you internalize,
the more you can make the changes to your shooting that
you need to make.

No matter what, don't quit. You can go anywhere you
want to go in the shooting sports, if you are willing to
work at it. It takes sacrifice, but if you decide it is important to you to get really good, you can make it happen.
I hope that this book helps get you there. I can tell you
from personal experience that buying a few books and
working with them can take you to the upper echelon of
the sport. You just need to do your part!

# GLOSSARY

**Alpha:** The maximum point-scoring zone on a USPSA/IPSC target

**Dry-fire:** Practicing with an unloaded firearm

**Group shooting:** Shooting a few shots in the same place on the target

**LASIK:** (Laser-Assisted in Situ Keratomileusis), commonly referred to as laser eye surgery

**Live-fire:** Actually firing a gun

**Magazine pouches:** Devices that hold magazines on your belt

**Magwell:** Device designed to aid reloading your firearm by making magazine insertion easier

**Open Division:** USPSA/IPSC division allowing for significant modifications to the competition firearm including optical sights

**Production Division:** USPSA/IPSC division using predominately unmodified firearms

**SIRT Pistol:** (Shot Indicating Resetting Trigger) A dry-fire training pistol to complement live-fire training

**Strong hand:** Your dominant hand

**Trigger freeze:** Attempting to pull the trigger so fast that you don't pull it far enough to discharge the gun

**Weak hand:** Non-dominant hand

**USPSA:** United States Practical Shooting Association

**IPSC:** International Practical Shooting Confederation

# ACKNOWLEDGMENTS

First, Ronnie Casper was again instrumental in making this book happen. He assembled the necessary photos, created diagrams, designed the cover, laid out, edited, uploaded, checked, rechecked, and proofed this book. Basically, he does all the really lame stuff that I lack the patience to do.

This book is the culmination of my personal shooting and learning journey. I have learned so much from so many people. It is simply impossible to recognize all of them. Shooters like Brian Enos, Rob Leatham, Mike Seeklander, Dave Sevigny, Matthew Mink, and many more have all been influential in my own development. I am sure the influence of these people is obvious.

I also need to thank all of the shooters that contributed material. Bob Vogel, Matthew Mink, Dave Sevigny, Jay Hirshberg, Matt Hopkins, JJ Racaza, Chris Bartolo, Keith Garcia, Blake Miguez, Brad Engmann, Mike Hughes, Taran Butler, Tim Herron, Nick Yanutola, Gaston Quindi Vallerga, Mike Foley, and Lori Casper all deserve my thanks.

The photographs included came from various sources:

Bob Vogel's photos were courtesy of Yamil Sued.
Matthew Mink's photos were courtesy of Rusty
    Hubbard.
Dave Sevigny's photos came from his wife, Brooke.
Keith Garcia's photo courtesy of James P. Mason—
    Aegis Atlanta.
Chris Bartolo provided his own photos.
Matt Hopkins provided his own photos.
Donna DeLambert provided photos.
Mark Miller provided photos.
JJ Racaza's photo is courtesy of Paul Erhardt.
Blake Miguez provided his own photo.
Mike Hughes provided his own photo.
Brad Engmann's photo was courtesy of Pat Johnson.
Lori Casper provided her own photo.
Tim Herron provided his own photos.
Nick Yanutola provided his own photo.
Taran Butler provided his own photo.
Mike Foley provided his own photos.
Jay Hirshberg provided his own photos.
Gaston Quindi Vallerga provided his own photo.

Finally, thanks to my lovely wife, Kita. She pushed my
shooting to the next level and pushed me to write this book.